INSIDE

Miss Jennie's Kitchen

RECIPES AND OTHER GIFTS FROM A DISTINGUISHED SOUTHERN FAMILY 1839 - 1965

by

Carolyn Ridenour

Happy Cooking and Pleasant Reading!
Carolyn Ridenour

McClanahan Publishing House

International Standard Book Number 0-913383 79 1
Library of Congress Catalog Card Number 2001092802

Cover design and book layout by James Asher Graphics

Manufactured in the United States of America

All book order correspondence should be addressed to:

Treetops Enterprises
1715 Stagecoach Rd.
Hanson, KY 42413

270-825-1533

treetops@spis.net

For

My mother, a good and faithful cook who permitted her kitchen, during the entire summer of 1963, to become a novice's laboratory

My brothers and late father, who served as guinea pigs that same summer

My late Aunt Anna Laura, who granted the preschooler her excess batter and pastry trimmings and planted a love for baking

Table of Contents

Acknowledgements

First and foremost I am indebted to my husband, Hugh, for his encouragement and insistence that I assemble this cookbook. Without his persistent urgings I would have forever held intentions of completing the project without ever finding or taking the time to do so. In addition, if not for his interest in the Green family history and his book, *The Greens of Falls of Rough, A Kentucky Family Biography 1795-1965*, I would never have known about Miss Jennie. He also gladly completed all technical, artistic, and business considerations required, leaving me only the pleasant tasks of recipe selection, translation, and composition. His advice and assistance were invaluable.

My thanks to Mary O'Neill, inheritor of the Green property and now a personal friend. She gifted me with the Green recipe collection as well as with several items from the Green dining room and kitchen. I cherish them all and, especially, her trust and friendship. She even "loaned" me her granddaughter, Jessica McGee, who has become a special part of my life and an enduring connection to Falls of Rough, Kentucky.

I am fortunate to have many supportive friends. Thanks to them all, and especially to Judi Wells, my most animated "encourager."

Author's Note

I must caution the reader that this is not the typical collection of recipes tested, retested, and updated to fit into the modern cook's repertoire. In fact, some of the recipes are ones that today's cook will have little interest in making, like mincemeat and sausage. However, I include them for their historical and educational merits. Not only would a historical cookbook be lacking without such recipes, but for me they are also much of the fascination of such a collection.

I *have* tested and experimented with some of the recipes–with mixed, but generally good, results. My only attempt to "update" them is to provide numerical guides for some temperatures and measurements. I also offer a table of equivalents, especially for archaic measurements and terms and for converting weight to volume measurements. And while some handwritten recipes, seemingly hastily recorded, required clarification, most retain their original wording. I have also kept the archaic spellings, punctuation usage, and sentence structures that characterized the older recipes. Significant in preserving historical integrity, they present, however, the problem of inconsistency when incorporated with the more current recipes. Like our food preparation processes, our language has changed much in the almost 150 years these recipes span. Here, for the sake of history, I sacrifice consistency.

To facilitate recipe use, I often rearranged the order of ingredients to correspond with mixing procedures. And for recipes–usually handwritten ones–without any instructions (early cooks were expected to know the rudiments), I sometimes added directions from similar recipes in the collection. At other times I left the method and procedure entirely to the reader. In such cases, the reader is on his or her own as something of a culinary pioneer for, excluding my experimentation, the recipes have lain idle for decades. Perhaps only through the lack of precision that characterized the recipes and kitchens of past eras can we fully appreciate the cook whose touch measured proper temperatures and whose eye determined appropriate amounts.

Carolyn Ridenour

Family Heritage

The Green Family (Jennie on steps) Early 1890s

Jennie at sixteen

Of Privilege and Mystery

"Miss Jennie." No last name is required to elicit a reaction from almost any long-standing resident in and around Falls of Rough, a small community located on the river boundary between Grayson and Breckinridge Counties in western Kentucky. The response is often the recounting of a personal story, sometimes first hand, but now more often one passed down from parents, grandparents, or other older relatives. Most of these adults can recall someone who either "knew" Miss Jennie or had some encounter with her. In fact, Jennie Green, the sole survivor of the Greens of Falls of Rough until her death in 1965, is something of an area folk figure–not because of any extraordinary characteristics, but because she and her family lived their lives so differently from their rural contemporaries.

While the neighbors, primarily poor farmers, managed a meager living from the hilly soil, the Greens owned the village of Falls of Rough and its several enterprises: a sawmill, gristmill, wool-carding mill, general store, and large farming operation. They decorated their home with the finest furnishings and employed maids, housekeepers, a cook, and a gardener. Well traveled, with destinations including exotic locations like Europe, China, and Japan, they filled their wardrobes with fashions from Louisville, New York, and Paris. Miss Jennie and her three brothers owned expensive automobiles, employed a chauffeur, and enjoyed frequent vacations away from "the Falls," the colloquial term for their small river village.

Jennie became more the focus of attention as she assumed responsibility for all the Green enterprises after her brothers–Willis, Preston, and Robert–died in the 1940s. Because she had given up her one-fourth inheritance in 1911, she had not been actively involved in the family's business or farm decisions since. Her resolution to do things her way, sometimes disregarding the expertise of the long-time experienced "hands," inspired discussion, especially as the businesses were already in decline and their survival of paramount concern. Though the ledgers confirmed less and less profit, Miss Jennie undertook a total redecoration of her home, changing it from a comfortable country home to what has been described as more of a museum.

For the next several years she continued her custom of spending most of her summers in the cooler climate of Wequetonsing, Michigan, or Chautauqua, New York. One summer she hired a special chauffeur to drive her on a tour of the eastern United States and on other occasions took trips to Costa Rica, Columbia, and Mexico. That comparatively extravagant lifestyle fostered a mysterious element that especially enveloped the eccentric spinster of the twenty-two-room manor house and contributed to sometimes highly imaginative speculations. The locals, curious about her destination and purpose whenever she departed Falls of Rough, wondered if she was meeting a suitor. Did she have another life outside Falls of Rough that she wished to keep secret? Without actual answers and unable to comprehend fully a lifestyle so in contrast with their own, they frequently contrived explanations.

More than three and a half decades after her death, narratives about her still abound–many, no doubt, speculative in origin and others greatly exaggerated due to years of retelling. But while her family's social and economic background set her apart early from those who lived around her, her age-enhanced eccentricities only added to her attraction as a subject of conversation. During roughly the last three decades of her life, she was preoccupied with the color of her name. She decorated with green, from her kitchen accessories to her linens and even her telephone. (In the 1950s when all others were black, she managed to have a green telephone.) Her clothing was almost exclusively green, including her shoes, and she owned what one local woman, then a child, described as "the only green fur coat I had ever seen before and have ever seen since." (It was actually a fur cape dyed a dark green.) Even her last automobiles were green.

However, one aspect of Miss Jennie's lifestyle clearly not speculation was her fondness for entertaining guests at her grand dining room table. Letters, thank-you notes, and interviews with a long-time cook as well as former guests offer proof. Even as late as the 1950s (she died at age eighty-five in 1965), a correspondent noted her insistence on treating day guests to lunch. Her kitchen holds bountiful tales, and her recipe collection helps to reveal a part of that lore.

Files, Folders, and Favorites

A few years ago I accompanied my historian husband to aid in his research of the historic Green family, founders of Falls of Rough. I was merely a helper–a reader of old letters and a peruser of old things. I never intended to be more. But letters, revealing and touching ones, have a way of pulling the reader inside them, just as the plot of a well-written story hooks and holds its audience. So, soon, I became an intruding observer–a "peeping Tom" of sorts–to a real life narrative of times past. A heretofore casual student of history, I now became immersed in the history of the Green family, especially in their everyday lives, their personalities, relationships, and motivations. In more than ten decades of personal letters, I found a real-life soap opera. What began as a chore became an anticipated treat. I read the family's correspondence voraciously–or as voraciously as antiquated handwriting and syntax allow. I was hooked.

One of the many advantages we enjoyed in this historic research is that the family home and much of the community the Greens founded still stands. When we began our investigation, the distant cousin who inherited the Green "home place" in 1965 still lived there. In addition, Mary O'Neill was kind, generous, and willing to allow our research to extend into the closets and drawers holding the documents and memorabilia that remained in the spacious 150 year-old manor house. All three generations of the Greens lived out their lives there; it was a historian's treasure.

When Mary learned of my interest in cookbooks, recipes, baking, and other things "kitchen," she most generously gifted me with the cookbooks and recipe collections from the family home. Some of the recipes date to the time of the first generation of Greens who moved to Falls of Rough in the early 1830s, Willis and Ann Green, Miss Jennie's great-uncle and aunt.

The Green recipe collection includes two large letter files made up of alphabetized pockets in what is actually a business accounts folder, one Jennie probably confiscated from the bookkeeper's office in the general store, located just a few yards from the manor house. Only one folder remains intact, its pockets filled with hundreds of recipes cut from newspapers and magazines, handwritten recipes in letters, on cards, stationery, scraps of bank statements, bills, receipts, and almost any other type of paper imaginable. Several brochures and booklets, some that accompanied new kitchen equipment (ice cream freezers, for example), also contain recipes for use with the products. In addition, several advertising brochures help fill the file pockets.

Also stored in the file are what appear to be the pages of a homemade cookbook–recipes cut from magazines and newspapers and pasted onto thick stationery sheets. These recipes seem to date from the late 1890s and, based upon the photos, articles, and advertising visible on the backs of some of the recipes, extend into the era of World War II. Each page carries one of eighteen headings in Miss Jennie's handwriting: "Breads," "Cakes," "Candies," etc. Most of these pages show extensive use. In addition, several sheets of the coarse stationery are straight-pinned together and, in the same handwriting, contain information she titled "Hints about canning." The instruction is basic and likely that of one just learning to "put by" foods. This evidence, combined with other clues, suggests that Jennie began preparing this collection as a novice shortly after she assumed household duties–first and tentatively after her mother's death in 1896 and then permanently after her father's death in 1907. Although evidence does not exist to reveal just how great or how sustained was the responsibility she undertook in the interval, a 1901 letter from her eldest brother, at home, to her younger brother in college verifies that Jennie was cooking for the family.

Another recipe assemblage fills a small wooden recipe box. Alphabetized dividers organize clipped and handwritten recipes, most of which seem to be from the 1930s and '40s. Like the other collections, this one is heavy with desserts, many for fancy and showy dishes. Brown paper sacks contain more recipes, mostly pages, columns, or single recipes from periodicals. If I did not know that Miss Jennie employed a cook most of her life, I would conclude that she loved to cook; however, I not only lack evidence to back up my theory, but almost all refutes it. Perhaps she gathered them for the use of her cook because she enjoyed trying new and different foods. Maybe, like her mother before her, she only hoped to delight her many guests.

Here I might add that numerous clipped or handwritten recipes of the collection were lost to time, moisture, or mice. Sometimes one or a combination of these elements affected only a word or number here or there, but rendered the recipes useless except for the most experimental of cooks. At other times those conditions stole only from the edges. I am grateful for the many recipes spared.

Three primary cookbooks–an 1842 edition of *Directions for Cooking* by Miss Leslie, an 1890 edition of *Housekeeping in Old Virginia*, and *The Hostess of To-day*, first published in 1899–show extensive use. The oldest has lost its cover as well as its last thirty-odd pages and shows great use in the "Sweetmeats" and "Pastry, Puddings, Etc." sections. All recipes in this book offer rudimentary directions in full prose style, as was the custom in early cookbooks. The *Old Virginia* cookbook remains in one piece, but barely. The last of the three, now literally in two parts, contains consecutively numbered recipes from 1 through 863, each of which gives the cost of making the dish. One large loaf of "Plain Cake," for example, cost "22 cts.," while the same loaf of "Delicate Cake" cost "25 cts.," the difference resting primarily in the number of eggs required. Two other books show less use: a 1933 edition of *Treasures of a Hundred Cooks* and a 1941 edition of *The Escoffier Cook Book*.

In choosing recipes to include here, I looked for evidence that a recipe had been used. For cookbooks, that meant finding pages stained and spattered or dog-eared. Many such pages contain multiple recipes; in that case I sometimes picked a representative one. At other times I relied on what I knew of Jennie's preferences–that she loved oysters, for example. Sometimes I simply guessed. I used the same spot-and-spatter test for the other recipes. Because I, too, sometimes clip recipes that I intend to try but never use, I looked for evidence that the recipe in question had at least been tried. Unlike my historian husband's more exacting criteria, mine are not historically sound. I hope the reader will forgive me this transgression.

Heritage and Heirlooms

Although the title of this book identifies the kitchen as belonging to Miss Jennie, I have to remind myself and the reader that it first belonged to

Jennie's Great-Aunt Ann, the Falls' first Mistress Green, and then to Jennie's mother, Ella. Because neither of these women ever moved away from the family home at Falls of Rough, their recipes and cookbook collections remained in the kitchen to become addenda to those of the subsequent mistress of the Green household.

In addition to the generational overlapping of recipes, the customs, habits, tastes, and methods of the earlier cooks surely influenced the latter ones. How many of us can deny the influence of our mothers' practices and preferences upon our own? How often have we heard relatives or friends wish for such and such prepared "the way Mom (or Grandmother) made it"? And even if, by rare chance, our mothers did not cook or were not adept in the kitchen, their menu selections certainly affected our tastes. With these facts in mind, I must acknowledge that in this cookbook we also go inside the kitchens of Miss Ella and Miss Ann, who not only left their portions of the recipe collection, but who also contributed their personal and culinary histories.

Family fare varied by season, but in Ann Green's kitchen fresh corn sometimes meant "a nice corn pudding every morning for breakfast," accompanied at times by fresh "tomatos with plenty of onions." Except for this reference in an 1868 letter, the handwritten portion of the collection reveals little data from Ann's kitchen. Some of the oldest recipes might have been hers, but no date or other identifying mark confirms it. During all of Ann's tenure as household mistress, from 1839 until the 1860s, food preparation occurred in the clapboard structure located about ten feet behind the manor house, where the huge open-hearth stone fireplace, approximately fifteen feet wide, likely provided the only source for cooking. Large pivoting iron cranes, staggered in height, offered room for several massive kettles and pots. By the late 1840s Willis Green owned twelve or thirteen slaves, one of whom likely served as the family cook. As a result, perhaps few recipes of that era were ever committed to paper, and the ones that were hide among those of the following two generations. The legacy of Miss Ann's kitchen rests primarily in the 1842 *Directions for Cooking* cookbook.

Jennie's mother, Ella, moved to the Falls of Rough manor house in 1866 when she married Jennie's father, Lafayette. And though Aunt Ann, who died in 1877, ran the household for almost forty years, she turned over her directorship of the kitchen to the new Mrs. Green soon after Ella's arrival. This transition did not happen quickly enough for Ella, however, who complained in a letter to her mother six years after her arrival that she wished soon to have "supreme control of the kitchen."

Ann Green

Ella spent much effort during her tenure as mistress at Falls of Rough trying to obtain and keep good cooks. It was not an easy task. While entertaining some of her husband's relatives shortly after her wedding, she was embarrassed by the cook's preparations and hoped that her fine china and silver presentation compensated for any shortcomings in the food. On another occasion she wrote of having to help the cook do much of the cooking when seven-year-old Jennie brought home from church "a raft of children" for dinner. At other times Ella had to assume full responsibility when a cook quit or was fired.

Although food preparation sometimes offered its troubles, variety and quantity of food were seldom problems in Ella's kitchen. One advantage of farm life was the abundance of fresh food in spring and summer. In general the Green family enjoyed a variety of foods, especially meats, because the farm produced cattle, sheep, goats, and hogs, with the latter meat generally in great supply. In November of 1887, Jennie's father butchered thirty-five hogs, afterward stating that he supposed the family would eat it instead of turkey for Thanksgiving. Young Jennie once exclaimed in a letter to a brother away at college, "We just finished hog killing and had a pig tail dinner." On occasion there was such an oversupply of meat that the children who were away from home received instruction to try to sell the surplus to the families of their friends and acquaintances.

Ella Green

What meats the farm could not supply were obtained from the surrounding countryside. Lafayette, often too busy to go hunting, contracted with local hunters to supply the table with wild game, agreeing to "supply the shot" in exchange for "half the kill." Rabbit with "real cream gravy" was one of Ella's specialties and a favorite of her many guests. There was also a plentiful supply of fish, primarily catfish, from the millpond, the source of waterpower for the several Green businesses.

Many other items such as fresh vegetables and eggs came from Ella's personal garden and her hen house filled with Plymouth Rock hens. She planted vegetables in hot beds to insure an early spring garden, which contained the standard vegetables along with raspberries and especially flowers, the latter a passion passed from mother to daughter Jennie. The surplus garden produce was typically canned or preserved in some form, as guests many times left with gifts of pickles or jams. In addition, the gristmill provided a ready store of freshly ground flour and cornmeal.

The more exotic items that could not be found on the Green estate were often available from Ella's parents, who maintained a home in Florida. The Greens often received shipments of fresh fruit, especially oranges or lemons, from her parents in exchange for some of their farm produce, such as country ham or maple sugar collected from the acres of maple forests and processed on the Green farm. Sometimes a family member passing through a large town like Owensboro or Louisville purchased a requested provision otherwise unavailable.

Sunday dinner was probably special for the Green family, as it was for many country people and as a menu found in a letter to a family member away from home attests. The meal consisted of "vegetable soup, saddle of mutton & vegetables & stewed pears & cake." Even though this was a Sunday dinner menu, the customary Green table must have been renowned. A family friend planning a visit to the Greens wrote to Ella requesting that she not go to any extra trouble preparing for his visit. He did, however, mention the "long and well filled dining room" as an anticipated attraction.

Ella surely brought with her to Falls of Rough recipes and preferences from her childhood Frankfort home and the kitchen dominated by her mother, Jennie's grandmother, Elizabeth Brown Scott, also well known for presenting a fine table. During most of her life, and especially in the early years of her marriage, Ella sought her mother's advice in weekly letters concerning almost every aspect of running a household. We know this fact not only from reading Mrs. Scott's letters to her, but also from Ella's letters to her mother, which became Ella's property upon her mother's death in 1886. Ella valued her mother's wisdom and, lamenting that she was too far away, often longed for the life she had known in Frankfort, Kentucky's capital city. What better way to sooth her yearnings than to prepare her mother's recipes and at the same time invoke memories of her home and family? Elizabeth Scott surely occupied the Green kitchen in her own indirect way.

Elizabeth Scott was the wife of Robert W. Scott, a prominent Bluegrass stock breeder and farmer. He ran a model farm just five miles from Frankfort with vegetable gardens, orchards, and animals that provided both fresh and cured meats. And although Elizabeth Scott had kitchen slaves to do the manual labor of cooking, she closely supervised the operation. On one occasion when expecting guests from Frankfort, she and the help began early to make preparations for their visit. When the anticipated guests did not arrive at the expected time, Mrs. Scott sent a servant to inquire of their whereabouts. Told they would not arrive until the next day, she again made preparations for a lavish meal. Turkeys and ducks were dressed, breads and vegetables readied, and the table set. Although Mrs. Scott was extremely annoyed by her visitors' lack of courtesy, she no doubt repeated the detailed

Elizabeth Scott

preparations for subsequent guests.

Like her mother, Ella took great pride in the products of her kitchen. She also realized the importance of the physical and social aspects of her home for their contribution to the enjoyment of family and friends who commonly became her guests. A great portion of the desired atmosphere revolved around the dining table, where "My Lady Green," as one frequent guest fondly referred to her, held a special reputation. No doubt a part of that reputation could be attributed to her well-equipped dining room: beautiful china, fine table linens, and an exquisite Tiffany silver service. After having excelled in her role as mistress of the Green home for thirty years, Ella died at age fifty-four in 1896.

Challenging Tasks

When young Jennie assumed responsibility for the household, she naturally inherited the use of her mother's nicely appointed dining facilities. She also acquired the high standards set by her mother and maternal grandmother, whom she had visited often as a child. In addition, as a young lady she had been a frequent guest in other homes like her own, where standard entertainment included lavish meals and parties. The task of fulfilling expectations must have seemed daunting to the seventeen-year-old Jennie when she first assumed partial household responsibilities upon her mother's death, as she also became a mother figure to her fourteen-year-old brother. Perhaps she was more prepared for the task eleven years later upon her father's death, when she truly became the third matriarch of the Green manor house.

Miss Jennie's kitchen—the actual room—was not meant for guests' eyes, unlike today's kitchen, which is often the hub of entertainment. Jennie's world, like that of her predecessors, was much more formal. So while her dining room was beautifully wallpapered and draped, gleaming with the rich wood tones of walnut and ash parquet floors and wainscoting, the kitchen was a true workroom for servants, with walls and floors of mere painted boards. In fact, the poorly equipped kitchen stood in stark–almost shocking–contrast to the elegance of the remainder of the house.

Originally separate from the manor house, the kitchen was eventually connected by a small room attached to the back hallway, probably in the late 1800s when cooking on an open hearth gave way to the first cook stoves and diminished the danger of cooking fires. A butler's pantry with access from the hallway opened onto the dining room. Here, one full wall provided glass-doored shelves at eye level and above, with storage cabinets below. A cast-iron sink on the opposite wall probably replaced a dry sink in the 1910s or '20s, and a small painted drop-leaf wooden table sat near the window in-between where, witnesses recall, the older Jennie preferred to take her meals when she dined alone. More food storage was available in the cellar, the entrance to which was originally just outside the back hall door. With the kitchen connected, access to the cellar moved conveniently indoors.

Like her mother, Jennie had difficulty finding and keeping good cooks, according to her correspondence. From the 1930s until her death in 1965, however, she managed to retain the same cook, Gwyn Spaulding, a wife and mother who grew up nearby and whose own young family eventually lived in a tenant house just behind the Green "mansion." In a 1978 interview the long-time cook remarked that working for Miss Jennie was a challenge because she was "hard to get along with" and difficult to please. Mrs. Spaulding further related that whenever a new girl was hired, she personally advised her to keep her suitcase packed. Most likely the new employee would not endure Jennie's demanding expectations or her less-than-diplomatic managerial style. Over the course of her thirty-plus years of employment, the faithful cook saw many potential employees arrive and then quickly depart. Some say Mrs. Spaulding's need for a home for her children, provided free by tenant housing, motivated her endurance as Miss Jennie's faithful employee and helps explain her longevity in the Green kitchen.

Shared Treasures

I never met Miss Jennie–did not really know about her until a decade or so ago, but I have since become immersed in her family's history. I am lucky to have some of her china, kitchen utensils, silver, and monogrammed table linens, not to mention a few pieces of her clothing and jewelry. And while owning her personal effects offers a tangible "Miss Jennie" connection, possessing her recipes in her own handwriting (or in the handwriting of her family or friends) adds another dimension. It offers an opportunity to share her experiences, an idea that excites me.

Hoping the reader appreciates my delight, I have included several facsimiles of the original recipes along with my translations. While I became especially familiar with Miss Jennie's "scribbles," an occasional deciphering mistake remains a possibility, for some of her handwritten recipes seem more a puzzle than otherwise. I invite the reader, before reading my translation, to apply his or her own deciphering skills to the originals, an activity that can itself be a sort of historical adventure.

I believe a look into the recipe file and cookbooks of a family tell much, not only about the family but also about the times. It is a part of history on the simplest, everyday plane. I am especially fortunate to be the beneficiary of such a wealth of recipes, so steeped in the well-documented history of three generations of an extraordinary Kentucky family. As one who enjoys her kitchen, I feel compelled to share that good fortune. I hope the reader gains a sense of history from this cookbook and, at the same time, finds some recipes that beg to be tried.

Beginnings

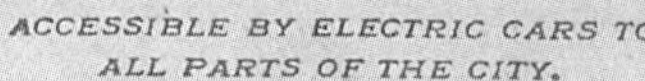

....The....
New Galt House Co.
INCORPORATED.
LOUISVILLE, KY.
W. S. MILLER, MANAGER.

EUROPEAN PLAN.

Helms Welsh Rarebit — 191

1 lb cheese put in chafing dis
with 1 ~~pt~~ cups cream
Stir until melted —
Then add the beaten yolks of 3
into which put 2 tablespoons
Worcestershire sauce red pepper
to taste and teaspoon salt
Cook until thick, serve on
crackers (unsalted) or toast —

Helms Welsh Rarebit

1 pound cheese
1 cup cream
3 egg yolks, beaten
2 tablespoons Worcestershire sauce
1 teaspoon salt
Red pepper

Stir together cheese and cream in a heated chafing dish until cheese melts. Add egg yolks, Worcestershire sauce, salt, and pepper to taste. Cook until thick. Serve on unsalted crackers or toast.

Creamed Oysters with Celery

Put three tablespoons of butter into a saucepan and as soon as it is hot add one cup of celery, cut in small pieces. Simmer for fifteen minutes, then add a half cup of oyster liquor, half cup of cracker crumbs, half cup of cream and salt and paprika to taste. Let this just come to a boil, then pour in a pint of oysters. Leave them long enough for the edges to curl, then serve on toast or saltines.

Oysters Fricassee

Put a tablespoon of butter in a frying pan, and as soon as it begins to brown add a half pint of well-drained oysters. When they commence cooking, stir in another tablespoonful of butter which has been mixed with a teaspoonful of flour. Cook one minute, add a teaspoonful of milk, salt, and paprika to taste, cook a moment longer and serve on toast or with hot rolls. If the oven is hot the rolls may be heated while the oysters are cooling. Put them in a paper bag, twist the open end tightly together and lay in the oven. Five or ten minutes heating this way makes them like freshly baked rolls.

Roquefort and Cream Cheese Balls

½ pound Roquefort cheese
1 small cream cheese
Butter the size of a walnut
½ teaspoon Worcestershire sauce
Dash of each: paprika, cayenne, salt
1 teaspoon minced olives

Blend the softened cheeses and butter; then add the seasonings by degrees. Add olives and form into balls with butter paddles; serve with salad.

FRANK B. WILLIAMS
RES. PHONE 519

MATTHEW H. GALT
RES. PHONE 450

WILLIAMS AND GALT
LAWYERS
NINTH FLOOR WOODRUFF BLDG
TELEPHONE 701
SPRINGFIELD, MISSOURI

Green salad with cheese

1 can pineapple — 1/2 cup sugar
3 lemons — 1 envelope Knox gel[illegible]
1 small cucumber — green vegetable coloring matter

Grated cheese & mayonnaise

To the juice of one can pineapple & 3 lemons add enough water to make a pint. Add sugar & bring to a boil. Dissolve gel[illegible] in this & add coloring matter to make a pretty green. When cool add 5 slices of pineapple diced & cucumber cut in small pieces. Put in [illegible] molds (small tea cups will do) & when serving cover thickly with grated cheese & mayonnaise.

Sweetbreads & cucumbers in tomato aspic

Boil sweetbreads blanch them & cut in small pieces. Dice cucumber. Put in individual mold 1/3 full of tomato aspic (any good recipe) & fill nearly to top with sweetbreads & cucumber mixed with well seasoned mayonnaise. Fill molds with aspic.

Green Salad with Cheese

1 can sliced pineapple, drained
3 lemons, juiced
½ cup sugar
1 envelope Knox gelatine
1 small cucumber, chopped
Green vegetable coloring water
Grated cheese
Salad dressing (or mayonnaise)

To the juice of one can pineapple and three lemons add enough water to make 1 pint. Add sugar and bring to a boil. Dissolve gelatine in sugar juices and add a few drops of coloring water. When cool add 5 slices of pineapple diced and cucumber cut into small pieces. Pour into individual molds (small teacups will do) and when serving cover thickly with grated cheese and mayonnaise.

Jell-O Lime Pepper Salad

½ package Lime Jell-0
¾ cup boiling water
1 tablespoon vinegar
3 cakes (9 ounces) cream cheese, softened
¼ teaspoon salt
⅛ teaspoon paprika
Dash of white pepper
2 medium-sized green peppers
Lettuce
Mayonnaise
Paprika

Dissolve Jell-O in boiling water, add vinegar, and chill. Meanwhile, combine cheese, salt, paprika, and white pepper; mix well. When Jell-O is slightly thickened, fold in cheese mixture; blend. Remove tops and seed peppers. Pour boiling water over them and let stand 1 minute. Drain and chill. Pour cheese mixture into peppers. Place in refrigerator in upright position. Chill until filling is firm. Cut in thin slices, using knife dipped in hot water. Serve on crisp lettuce. Garnish with mayonnaise and paprika. Serves 6.

Miss Jennie (or her cook) must have been pleased when lime Jell-O became available in 1930. This recipe, clipped from a magazine and accompanied by a brightly colored illustration of the dish, includes the note "(Made with the new flavor-Lime)." No longer would "green vegetable coloring matter" need to be added to the gelatin in order to achieve the effect with which Jennie seemed so preoccupied.

Crab Salad

1 cupful mayonnaise
½ cupful chili sauce
1 hard-cooked egg yolk, chopped
1 tablespoonful stuffed olives, chopped
1 tablespoonful green pepper, diced
1½ ounce can caviar
½ pound fresh crab meat
Lettuce

Make a salad dressing by mixing well the first six ingredients. Add the crab meat and serve on a bed of lettuce.

FLORIDA SANITARIUM
AND HOSPITAL
MEDICAL AND SURGICAL

GUESTS' STATIONERY ORLANDO, FLO

Savory Cheese Salad

1 envelope Knox Gelatin

1/4 cup cold water

1/4 cup mild vinegar

1/2 cup stuffed olives chopped

1 cup boiling water

1/3 cup cream (whipped)

1/2 teaspoon salt

1 1/2 cup grated American ch

1/2 cup celery chopped

1/4 cup green pepper

When gelatin begins to cool & until jelly — fold in all ingredients — mold in ice — good for sandwich fillings

Savory Cheese Salad

1 envelope Knox gelatin
¼ cup cold water
¼ cup mild vinegar
½ cup stuffed olives, chopped
1 cup hot water
⅓ cup cream, whipped
¼ teaspoon salt
1½ cup grated American cheese
½ cup celery, chopped
¼ cup green pepper, chopped

Dissolve gelatin and water and allow to cool. When gelatin begins to thicken, beat until frothy. Fold in all remaining ingredients. Mold on ice. (good for sandwich fillings)

At Falls of Rough the Greens had an icehouse located approximately fifty yards from their residence. Each winter, ice was cut in large blocks from the frozen river and packed with sawdust to help preserve it for household use until the next year's winter freeze. Because the river was frozen deeper than usual in January 1884, filling the icehouse required ten workmen several hours just to saw the ice. That year, in fact, the farm manager had to borrow a larger saw to complete the task.

Pear and Cream Cheese Salad

Ripe pears
Lime or lemon juice
1 small cream cheese, softened
4 tablespoons chili sauce
Mayonnaise
Cream (about ½ cup)
Blanched almonds (4 per serving)

Peel, core, and halve enough pears to allow for number of servings required. Allow to marinate in lime or lemon juice for ½ hour before filling. Mix cream cheese and chili sauce and fill centers of pears. Mix mayonnaise and enough cream to thin; beat well together just before serving and pour over filling. Garnish each pear half with almonds.

Tomato-Salad Dressing

1 can tomato soup
¾ cupful vinegar
½ cupful oil
¼ cupful sugar
1 tablespoon Worcestershire Sauce
3 tablespoons grated onion
1 teaspoon salt
1 teaspoon paprika
1 scant teaspoon ground mustard

Into a quart jar place the first six ingredients in the order given. Combine the salt, paprika and mustard and add to the first mixture. Seal and shake well. This dressing is good on head lettuce and will keep for a month in the refrigerator. Stir before each use.

Corn Salad

1 dozen ears corn
4 sweet green peppers, chopped
4 sweet red peppers, chopped
1 head cabbage, shredded
1 stalk celery, chopped
5 small white onions, chopped
1 quart vinegar
2 cups sugar
2 heaping teaspoons dry mustard, dissolved in a little vinegar
1 tablespoon salt

Cut kernels from cobs and combine with remaining vegetables. Mix vinegar, sugar, mustard, and salt; blend well and pour over vegetables. Cook for 20 minutes and then allow to cool. Cover and store in the ice-box.

Dandelion Salad

3 quarts fresh dandelion greens
6 eggs, hard boiled
1 teaspoonful salt
1 teaspoonful pepper
2 dessertspoonfuls vinegar
3 dessertspoonfuls olive oil
1 tablespoonful finely chopped pickles

Cut all the tender parts of the greens in such a way that there is a small heart in each part, about three or four leaves in each. Mash the yolks of three eggs (save the whites for another use) with the remaining ingredients and blend well. Wash and drain dandelions and mix thoroughly with yolk mixture. Slice remaining three eggs and place them on top; garnish with nasturtium blossoms, if desired.

Molded Avocado Salad

For the first, add to a package of mint gelatine (at syrupy stage) a paste made of one large mashed avocado and cream cheese softened with top milk and mayonnaise, and flavored with cayenne, lemon juice, and salt. Mold as usual and serve with mayonnaise. This salad is especially good as a delicacy subterfuge when avocadoes are high because it will serve ten people. The amount can be varied by the amount of gelatine used.

Tom Davis, eldest son of Miss Jennie's long-time chauffeur of the same name, recalled that the last Lady Green returned from almost every trip to Louisville with several avocadoes, a fruit not available in or near her rural community—and an oddity to the young Davis. He remembered that Miss Jennie enjoyed them simply cut in half and served fresh.

Vegetables & Side Dishes

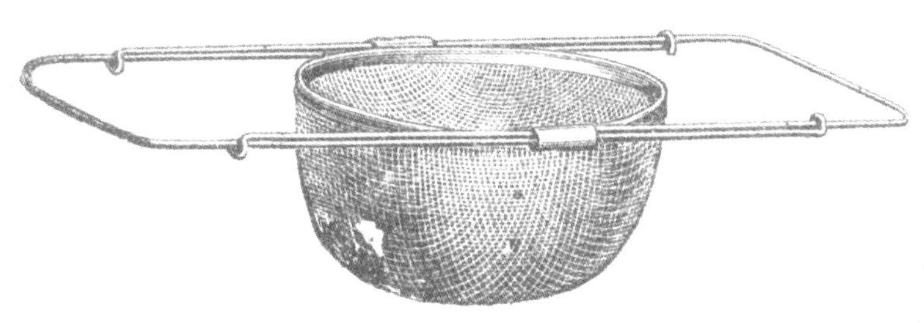

Green Corn Pudding

1 quart fresh whole milk
¼ pound butter, melted
¼ pound sugar
4 eggs, beaten till quite light
12 ears of green corn, grated

Stir into the milk by degrees the butter and sugar. Then add the eggs alternately with the grated corn, and pour into a large buttered dish. Bake four hours. This dish may be eaten either warm or cold. If desired, serve with sauce: Beat together equal portions of butter and sugar with ground nutmeg added to taste.
Note: Green corn is defined in this recipe as "Indian corn when full grown, but before it begins to harden and turn yellow."

Ann Green wrote in 1868 that fresh corn meant "a nice corn pudding every morning for breakfast," accompanied at times by fresh "tomatos with plenty of onions."

Potato Snow

Peel and boil in a saucepan, six large mealy white potatoes. Add a little salt to the water. Take them out one by one, leaving the saucepan on the fire. Rub through a sieve into a deep dish, letting it fall in a mound. Do not touch with a spoon or the hand. Have a sauce-boat of melted butter to serve with it at the table.

To Cook Inferior Sweet Potatoes

Boil till nearly done. Cut in thick slices; put a layer in the bottom of a baking dish. Put pepper, salt, sugar, bits of butter, and a teaspoonful vinegar on this layer, and so on till the dish is filled, leaving a layer of seasoning for the top. Pour over it a teacup rich milk. Put a tin plate on top and bake a few minutes. Put grated cracker, on top.

Chicago Hot (Tomatoes put up

One peck ripe tomatoes
2 cups of onions
2 cups of celery
5 red peppers
5 green peppers
all cut fine strain all the juice off using only pulp & mix with the other ingredients
2 cups sugar.
3 cups Vinegar
1/2 cup salt
2/3 3/4 cup mustard seed
put in fruit jars and sea

Chicago Hot Tomatoes

1 peck ripe tomatoes
2 cups onions
2 cups celery
5 red peppers
5 green peppers
2 cups sugar
3 cups vinegar
½ cup salt
¾ cup mustard seed

Finely cut all the vegetables and strain. Mix only the pulp with the remaining ingredients and seal in fruit jars.

Stuffed Tomatoes

Tomatoes, fresh whole
Milk
1 slice stale bread
Anchovies
Tuna fish
Garlic
Parsley
Tarragon leaves
Pepper
Bread crumbs
Olive oil

Scoop pulp from tomatoes. Soak bread slice in milk and then press dry. Mix bread with fish and seasonings and stuff into prepared tomatoes. Cover with bread crumbs, sprinkle with olive oil, and place under the broiler for 15 minutes.

Note: Jennie must have enjoyed this dish on one of her excursions, as she wrote it on an invitation to the Piccadilly Club while a guest at the Mount Royal Hotel in Banff, Canada. It seems more an answer to "What's in this tomato?" than otherwise. She later copied it with clearer wording (though still no amounts) onto plain notepaper.

Asparagus Soufflé with White Sauce

4 tablespoonfuls flour
4 tablespoonfuls butter
⅔ cupful milk
¼ cupful grated cheese
Salt and pepper
1 one-pound can asparagus
3 eggs, separated

Mix the first three ingredients and cook till thick. Then add the cheese and season with salt and pepper to taste. Stir until smooth and set aside.

Heat the asparagus and put through a sieve. Add this to the white sauce and return it to the stove. Beat the egg yolks, add to the mixture, and take from the fire at once. Beat the egg whites till stiff and gently fold in. Pour the entire mixture into a well-greased baking dish, set in a pan of hot water, and bake in a slow oven until firm in the center.

Egg-Plant Farci

3 very small egg-plants
1 cup bread crumbs, divided
½ cup cooked chicken, veal, or lamb
1½ cups stock, divided
3 tablespoons butter, divided
⅛ teaspoon salt
Dash of each: pepper, nutmeg
1 egg, beaten
¼ cup white wine
1 tablespoon flour
1 tablespoon sherry

Boil egg-plants 20 minutes and drain. Then cut each one in half lengthwise; scoop out inside, leaving shell ½ inch thick. Mix ½ cup breadcrumbs, meat, ½ cup stock, 1 tablespoon butter, spices, and egg, and fill the egg-plant halves. (The pulp of the egg-plant may be used instead of meat, if desired.) Place in a baking pan. Combine the remaining 1 cup stock with the wine and pour in pan with the egg-plants. Bake 1 hour, basting often. Then cover with ½ cup breadcrumbs that have been browned in 1 tablespoon butter and place vegetables on a hot serving dish. Combine 1 tablespoon butter with the flour and cook until smooth; add 1 cup liquor from baking pan and the sherry. Mix well, pour around egg-plants, and serve.

In 1945 Maydee Crawford and Pauline Beauchamp moved to Falls of Rough, where their stepfather worked as a farm hand for the Greens. As they became preteens and older, Miss Jennie frequently hired them to serve her luncheon or dinner guests and sometimes to baby-sit her guests' children while the adults socialized. They recalled that among her favorite menu items were strawberry with rhubarb pie and stuffed eggplant.

To Dress Cucumbers Raw

Gather early in the morning, peel, lay in cold water till just before dinner. Then drain, slice as thin as possible into ice water, which drain and then fill a dish with alternate layers of sliced cucumber and thinly sliced white onion, sprinkled with salt and pepper. Pour a cup of weak vinegar over it and lay a lump of ice on top.

Spiced Peaches

Take nine pounds ripe peaches, rub them with a coarse towel, and halve them. Put four pounds sugar and one pint good vinegar in the kettle with cloves, cinnamon, and mace. When the syrup is formed, throw in the peaches a few at a time; when clear, take them out and put in more. Boil the syrup till quite rich; pour it over the peaches. Cherries can be pickled in the same way.

Jennie, 1905-1910

Hollandaise Sauce

3 egg yolks at room temperature
2 tablespoons cold water
1 tablespoon lemon juice
½ cup melted unsalted butter, somewhat cooled
Salt to taste
Cayenne pepper to taste

Put egg yolks in saucepan; add water and lemon juice. Cook on low heat, stirring constantly until the consistency of cream. Remove from heat and add a tablespoon of butter at a time. (Butter should be same temperature as eggs.) Season with salt and a dash of cayenne pepper. (By adding cream, this becomes sauce Musselein.*)

Note: Hollandaise Sauce, though sometimes tricky to make, is great for turning a simple vegetable or meat dish into a super one. Some modern recipes recommend cooking this sauce in a double boiler.
*This is Miss Jennie's misspelling of *Mousseline*, a variation served with vegetables or fish.

Jellied Apple Sauce

2 cups apple sauce
½ cup sugar
2 tablespoons red cinnamon candies
½ teaspoon nutmeg
1 teaspoon gelatin
2 tablespoons water
1 teaspoon lemon juice

Heat apple sauce to boiling point, and add sugar, candies, and nutmeg. Soak gelatin in cold water; add to apple sauce mixture, stirring until gelatin is dissolved. Cool. Add lemon juice and turn into mold. Chill until firm. Serve with pork, chicken, or duck.

Main Dishes

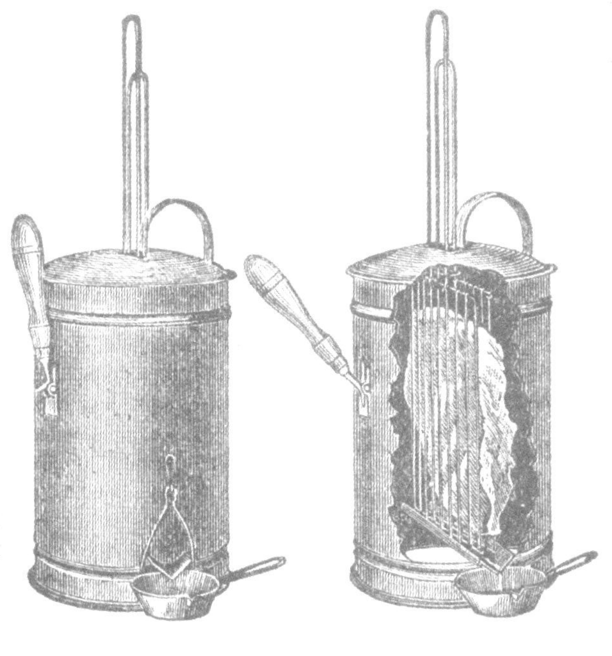

To Cook and Keep A Cured Ham

Soak the ham in cold water for 12 to 14 hours, adding 2 tablespoons of brown sugar to the water in which the ham is to be cooked. Simmer from 15 to 20 minutes to each pound. Allow the ham to cool in the water in which it has been cooked. Remove the skin carefully so as not to tear the fat. Sprinkle with brown sugar, black pepper or paprika, stick in oven and baste with sherry or vinegar sauce and bake just long enough to get a rich golden brown color. Serve either hot or cold. To keep the ham, retain the skin and use it as a covering for the ham after each carving to keep it from drying and to protect it from dust, etc. Wrap heavy, clean coarse cloths or cup towels around ham when it is not being used and put in cool place. Paraffin paper may be wrapped around ham to keep it juicy and clean. Never leave it exposed while not in use.

Planked Steak

For this purpose have a hard, well-seasoned oak plank. Rub it well with butter and set in the oven until very hot. Lay on it a thick, juicy steak, and fasten this in place by pushing several thumbtacks securely into the edges. Rub the steak with butter, and set in the oven, on the upper grating. Cook until done, rubbing with butter every few minutes. Lay the plank with the steak on it upon a huge platter, season with melted butter, pepper and salt to taste and arrange about it Parisian or French-fried potatoes.

Baked Apples Stuffed with Sausage Meat

6 large tart apples
1 cup sausage meat
Sugar

Scoop out centers of fresh apples, leaving a thick shell and being careful not to pierce the stem end while removing core. Cut all the pulp possible from the core, or sacrifice another apple to get the same quantity. Partially cook the sausage and mix it with the chopped apple. Sprinkle apple centers with sugar to taste and fill with sausage mixture, heaping it well. Bake in a medium hot oven until apples are tender. Serve with baked or creamed potatoes and corn bread.

Common Sausage-Meat

6 pounds lean, young, fresh pork
3 pounds fat of pork
9 teaspoonfuls of each: pepper, salt
Dried sage powder (3 teaspoonfuls per pound of meat)

Combine thoroughly together the lean and fat meat; add pepper and salt and then strew on the sage. Mix the whole very well with your hands. Put it in a stone jar, packing it down hard, and keep it closely covered. Set the jar in a cool dry place.

To make this a *fine* sausage, use leg meat and allow 2 pounds of fat to 3 of lean. Add 30 cloves, a dozen blades of mace powdered, three grated nutmegs, and 2 tea-spoonfuls of powdered rosemary in addition to the salt, pepper, and sage in the recipe for common sausage.

Pork Tenderloin with Sweet Potatoes and Apples

Tenderloin(s)
Poultry dressing (highly seasoned)
Minced onion
Butter, melted
Flour
Sweet potatoes, parboiled
Red apples
¼ cup butter, cold
4 tablespoons brown sugar
1 teaspoon salt

Having chosen amounts appropriate to serving needs, cut the tenderloin(s) lengthwise but do not quite separate. Open, flatten, and then spread with the dressing and onion. Put the halves back together, sandwich fashion, and fasten securely with a string. Rub with melted butter and dredge lightly with flour. Put in baking pan and surround with sweet potatoes, peeled and halved. Add cored and quartered (but not peeled) apples. Dot apples and potatoes thickly with butter and sprinkle with brown sugar and salt. Bake until the tenderloins are done and the potatoes golden brown; remove the string. Serve on a hot platter, meat in center, the potatoes and apples alternating as border. If desired, make gravy from pan drippings.

In a letter dated December 6, 1897, Jennie's father wrote to her fifteen-year-old brother in Louisville: "We did not keep Thanksgiving day as a holiday, as we had too much work to do, did not have any turkey or anything extra for dinner. We killed hogs last week and are now eating fresh hog meat with hominy."

Game-

th[illegible] The red fle[illegible]
a[illegible]s [illegible] ...mplating,
fully [illegible]ked [illegible] wholesome
digest[illegible] All me[illegible] hould be quickly [illegible]
at first. [illegible]is sears the outside and retains
the flavo. and juices. The after-cooking may
[illegible] wly, especially with white-fleshed
birds, [illegible] and chicken. Game is best
cooked quickly a[illegible] ved at once.

There is quite a difference in quality and flavor of wild ducks. The canvasback and [re]dhead ducks are always best cooked with[out] stuffing; it seems a pity to stuff these fine [bir]ds. Mallards, teals, widgeons and wood-ducks may be stuffed with rice, hominy or potatoes nicely seasoned with chopped English walnuts. Canvasbacks and redheads are vegetable eaters, hence the flavor is sweet and palatable.

Opossum

SKIN, singe and wipe the opossum insid[e] and out, then hang in a cold place fo[r] several days. Boil and mash four good-size[d] white potatoes; add a cupful of black walnut[s] chopped fine; add a teaspoonful of salt, a gra[t]ing of onion, and a dash of peppe[r] [illegible] opossum, sew it up, place it in t[illegible] pan, pour over a quart of boiling wa[ter] [illegible] stock, dust with salt and pepper, and [illegible] for three hours, basting frequently. Hav[e] the oven very hot at first, then cool it dow[n] to about 240° Fahrenheit. Serve with [illegible] kale or spinach and panned baked ap[illegible] apple sauce and cornbread.

Bengal Curry

CUT two young chickens [illegible] same as for fricassee. P[illegible] meat and bony pieces in the botto[m] [illegible] saucepan, the white meat on [illegible] with boiling water, bring quickly [illegible] and simmer gently for one ho[ur] [illegible] chopped onion, a bay leaf, a teasp[oonful] [of] salt, and simmer for thirty minutes lo[nger]. The chicken must be very tender. [Rub] through a sieve one can of Spanish [illegible] peppers; do not use any of the oil in w[hich] they are canned. Rub together a t[able]spoonful of butter and two of flour; add a pint of water in which the chicken [was] boiled, and the peppers that have been pr[essed] through a sieve; add half a cupful of t[illegible] stewed tomatoes, and stir the whole un[til it] reaches the boiling point. Put two tea[spoon]fuls of curry in a bowl, add just a little [illegible] to moisten; add this to the other sauce [illegible] add grated onion. Cook, [st]irring con[stantly] for five minutes. Take from the [illegible] add half a cupful of thick cream and [illegible] tablespoonful of butter. Lift the p[ieces of] chicken, put them in the sauce, sta[nd] [in] hot water covered closely for at le[ast] [illegible] minutes. Serve in a deep dis[h] [illegible] with dry, plain, boiled rice.

Chicken Croquettes
~~Chop~~ sufficient cold
boiled chicken to make
a qt. add to it two
teaspoonful of salt - two
tbls. of parsley - 1 tabl. grated
onion - 1 teasp. red pepper
mix thoroughly. Put into
a pt. of milk - add to it
rubbed to a smooth paste
tablespn of butter & four
of flour - stir until smooth
and thick - add chicken - mix
and turn out to cool - form into
croquettes - dip in egg - roll in crumbs
fry in hot fat - serve with tomato sauce

Chicken Croquettes

Cold boiled chicken meat (enough to make one quart), chopped
2 teaspoons salt
2 tablespoons chopped parsley
1 tablespoon grated onion
1 teaspoon red pepper
1 pint milk, scalded
2 tablespoons butter
4 tablespoons flour
2 eggs, beaten
2 cups crushed cracker crumbs
Oil for frying

fore Lafayette, nnie's father, ilt his wife a icken house, Ella plained in an 1867 tter to her parents hat she was glad er Falls of Rough eighbors exchanged hickens and eggs

for dry goods at the Greens' general store. She complained that she could raise no poultry due to the large population of minks in the area.

Add salt, parsley, onion, and red pepper to chicken and mix thoroughly. Make a paste of butter and flour; add some of hot milk to paste to mix and then add all to remaining hot milk. Cook over low heat, stirring constantly, until milk mixture is smooth and thick. Add chicken; mix well and turn out to cool. Form into croquettes; dip into eggs and then roll in crumbs. Fry in hot oil.

Note: This was a long-time family favorite. It is handwritten in two locations in Miss Jennie's homemade cookbook.

In a letter dated April 4, 1901, Jennie's older brother Willis wrote to her youngest brother, Robert, in college: "Sister is in the kitchen cooking as we have no cook and no prospect of one."

Chicken with Chestnut Purée

2 young chickens (about 4 pounds)
Lard
Chestnut dressing (recipe follows)
2 cups hot chicken stock (or water)
2 cloves
3 pepper-corns
½ teaspoon salt
1 sprig parsley
1 tablespoon hot butter
2 tablespoons flour
1½ cups liquor from pan
Chestnut purée (recipe follows)

Lard breasts of chickens and stuff with dressing. Combine stock, cloves, pepper-corns, salt, and parsley; pour over chickens and simmer 15 minutes. Then place chickens in baking dish, dredge with flour, and bake in hot oven 1½ hours, basting often. Combine butter, flour, and pan liquor; cook to brown. Place baked chickens on a hot serving dish and pour gravy over all. Surround with chestnut purée and serve.

Chestnut Dressing

1 cup chestnut meats
Salt to taste
2 tablespoons butter
1 tablespoon cream
¼ teaspoon salt
Dash cayenne
1 nutmeg, grated
½ cup bread-crumbs
2 tablespoons hot water

Boil chestnuts in salted water for 20 minutes (or until tender), drain, and mash. Combine remaining ingredients and add to nuts. Mix well and use to stuff turkey or chicken.

Chestnut Purée

1 quart chestnuts, shelled
2 tablespoons cream
2 tablespoons butter
¼ teaspoon each: salt, paprika, onion-juice

Blanch and boil chestnuts until soft; press through a colander. Add remaining ingredients and mix thoroughly. Press through a potato-ricer and serve.

Fricasseed Rabbit

2 rabbits, cut up
Seasonings to taste: cayenne pepper, salt, chopped parsley, powdered mace
1 pint veal broth (optional)
Butter
Flour

Gravy

1 jill or more thick cream
Ground nutmeg

Put rabbit pieces in a stew pan; season to taste with pepper, salt, parsley, and mace. Pour in veal broth or substitute warm water. Stew over low heat, adding some bits of butter rolled in flour when meat is about half cooked. Cook until meat is tender. Just before removing from heat, pour in cream, to which has been added the nutmeg (to taste). Stir the gravy well, but do not let it boil. Put meat on hot dish and pour gravy over all.

In an undated letter, likely from the 1880s, a potential guest of Jennie's mother acclaimed Ella's "rabbits with real cream gravy."

Creamed Chicken

2 tablespoons butter
3 tablespoons arrowroot or flour
½ cup hot milk
Chicken stock (thick)
1 cup cream or rich milk
½ teaspoon salt
Dash cayenne pepper
1 teaspoon parsley, minced
¼ teaspoon Kitchen Bouquet or grated nutmeg
2 cups cooked chicken or 1½ cups chicken and ½ cup mushroom and two truffles
Bread crumbs, buttered and browned

Cook butter and arrowroot thoroughly; add milk, chicken stock, cream, and seasonings. Add chicken and fill individual, greased ramekins; cover with crumbs. Bake 5 minutes.

Note: This recipe from *The Hostess of To-day* has one of Jennie's penciled *X's* beside it, a sure sign of her selection as a favorite. The dish cost 60 cents to make at the time of the cookbook's publication and was touted as a good one for the chafing dish.

Roast Duck with Dressing

On June 16, 1959, Bart Brown, trust officer of Louisville's Citizens Fidelity Bank, wrote to thank Miss Jennie for "the fine duck dinner."

Ducks
Salt
White bread crumbs
Minced onion, to taste
Butter
Minced parsley or chopped celery
Sage, salt, pepper, or poultry dressing

Singe ducks well and wash thoroughly. After dressing, salt them inside and outside and put on ice over night. Rinse very thoroughly in cold water. Now they are ready to stuff as you would any fowl. Cut the giblets into small pieces, and boil until done before adding to the gravy. Brown the ducks slightly; then cover the roaster and roast about one hour or until the legs are tender. This method produces a very mild flavor.

Dressing: Sauté bread crumbs, crushed fine, with the minced onion in butter until all is a rich brown. Use the amount of onion you like, but it's a safe rule to say use *plenty*, as the flavor goes into the bird and will not be offensive in the dressing. Add 2 cupfuls minced parsley to each quart of crumbs (after they are fried). Then add sage, salt, and pepper or poultry seasoning and enough to *moisten* (not wet) the dressing. If you wish celery dressing, use the same proportions of ingredients, substituting celery for the parsley. Season highly and to taste.

Breads

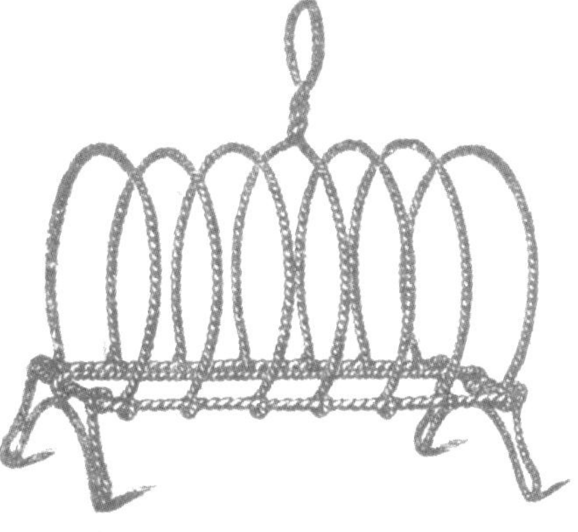

Some Bread-Making Tips

* Strong fresh yeast from the brewery should always be used in preference to any other.
* If using homemade yeast, increase recipe amount by half or, perhaps, double. If the homemade yeast is not very strong or fresh, you may need to treble the recipe quantity.
* If the flour is cold, warm it.
* When dough is to be made into rolls or fancy forms, it needs to be a little stiffer than for loaves.
* Dough should only half fill the baking pan.
* Allowing loaf dough to rise more than double risks its falling during the baking.
* Unlike loaves, rolls should rise to slightly more than double, and the oven should be hotter, browning 1 teaspoon of flour in 1 minute.
* Bread made of milk instead of water, and with shortening, is more tender than when water alone is used.
* The goodness of bread depends much on the kneading, which to do well requires strength and practice.
* In winter, place the bowl of rising dough nearer the fire than in summer.
* Unless you have other things to bake at the same time, it is not worth while to heat a brick oven for a small quantity of bread.
* Try the heat of the bottom of a brick oven by throwing in some flour; if it scorches and burns black, do not venture to put in the bread till the oven has had some time to become cooler. If a teaspoon of flour browns

in 5 minutes, the heat is right.
* Warm water that has had pumpkin boiled in it is very good for making bread.
* Prepare cloths for wrapping bread by sprinkling them plentifully with water, and letting them lie awhile rolled up tightly. This will make the crust of the bread less dry and hard.
* Bread should not be put in the breadbox until it is entirely cold.

Homemade Yeast

Boiling water
1 cup sweet milk
1 scant teaspoon sugar
1 scant teaspoon salt
Flour

Early in the morning: Add enough boiling water to the milk so that the mixture is tolerably hot. Stir in the sugar, salt, and enough flour to thicken. Place in a vessel of hot water and keep hot for five to six hours, when it will be light and ready to use in bread making.
Note: Six hours might not be sufficient, so let patience rule for this recipe, whose "fragrance" belies taste.

Quicker Homemade Yeast

1 cup sweet milk
Cornmeal

The morning <u>previous</u> to baking day, stir into a large cup of milk enough cornmeal to thicken by cooking it. Put in a warm place until <u>the next morning</u> when it will be light enough to make bread.

Jennie's father wrote in a December 6, 1897, letter to her youngest brother, away from home in Louisville: "We have the new flour mill running, and it is doing well, making beautiful flour, a sample which I will send up soon."

Common Rolls

2 pounds flour
1 teaspoon salt
1 jill water
1 jill milk
1 jill fresh yeast

Mix flour and salt in a large pan. Combine water and milk, and heat to just warm; add yeast. Make a hole in the middle of the pan of flour and pour liquid mixture into it. Mix into the liquid enough of the flour to make a thin batter, which you must stir till quite smooth and free from lumps. Then strew a handful of flour over the top, and set it in a warm place for two hours or more. When it is quite light, and has cracked on the top, make it into a dough with some more milk and water. Knead well for 10 minutes. Cover and allow to rise for 20 minutes in a warm place. Then make the dough into rolls or round balls. Bake in a square pan in moderate oven till lightly browned. Send them to table hot, cut in three, buttered and put together again.

Rolls

4 cups flour
1 cup milk luke warm [illegible]
1/2 cup luke warm water
dissolve 1 cake yeast in water
1 tablesp. sugar
1 teasp. salt
1/2 cups lard or part butter
mix & roll
rise [illegible] put in frigidaire [illegible]
make out in rolls rise 1 1/2 [illegible]

Scotch Short Bread

1 cup of butter
1 " " brown sugar
2 1/2 cups of flour
roll dry then [illegible]
[illegible] water
[illegible] pan [illegible]
1 [illegible]

Rolls

¼ cup lukewarm water
1 cake yeast
4 cups flour
1 cup lukewarm morning milk
1 tablespoon sugar
1 teaspoon salt
½ cup lard or part butter

Dissolve yeast in warm water, and then mix in all ingredients well. Allow to rise 2 hours and put in refrigerator until time for baking. Make out in rolls; allow to rise 1½ hours. Bake till lightly browned.

Potato Yeast Muffins

1 large potato
½ cup milk, scalded
1 tablespoon butter
½ teaspoon salt
½ tablespoon sugar
1 egg
1 cake yeast
2 cups flour

Boil potato, peel, and put through a sieve or mash fine (almost 1 cup). Blend scalded milk with potato; blend in butter, salt, sugar, and well-beaten egg. Cool to 80° and add yeast, stirring to dissolve. Sift flour before measuring. Add all flour to liquid and mix in thoroughly. Knead until smooth and set to rise in a greased bowl until dough doubles in bulk, about one hour. Then punch down and let rise fifteen minutes at 80°. Divide dough into twelve pieces; shape into balls and place in greased muffin pan. Let rise until double in bulk, about twenty minutes. Bake to a light brown.
Note: If using active dry yeast, sprinkle 2¼ teaspoons into the potato/milk mixture when it has cooled to between 105° and 115° F.

Salt Rising Bread

1 cup milk, scalded (but not boiled)
1 teaspoon salt
2 teaspoons sugar, divided
Corn meal
1 quart warm water
Flour

Mix milk, salt, 1 teaspoon sugar, and enough meal to make a thick mush. Beat and let stand in a warm place overnight. In the morning add warm water and 1 teaspoon sugar. (The water must not be hot, but comfortably warm to bear the finger.) Add enough flour to produce the consistency of pancake batter and let rise. When light, add flour enough to knead. Mold into loaves; let rise again, and bake from 40-60 minutes.

Corn Fritters

8 large ears of corn, cut three times (not grated)
2 eggs
1 teacup sweet milk (or more, if the corn is not juicy)
Salt and pepper to taste

Make the mixture the consistency of soft batter and fry in lard or butter.

Soda Crackers

1 quart flour
1 tablespoonful lard and butter mixed
1 egg
A little salt
1 teaspoonful soda, sifted into the flour
Buttermilk

Mix all ingredients and make a stiff paste with buttermilk. Beat until light, roll tolerably thin, cut in squares, prick, and bake quickly.

Cornmeal Batter Cakes

1 cup cornmeal
¼ tablespoon salt
1 tablespoon sugar
¼ teaspoon soda
2 tablespoons butter, melted
1¼ cups sour milk

Combine the dry ingredients and then add the liquid ones. Immediately pour (as you would pancake batter) onto a hot, oiled griddle or skillet. Cook until top looks set; flip to lightly brown second side. Serve immediately with extra butter and syrup, if desired.

Note: Omit soda if you wish to use sweet milk instead of sour milk.

George Bickle of Louisville, who was elected president of the Pendennis Club there in 1945, wrote in September 1939 that his "sweet tooth was completely satisfied by the delicious maple syrup" Jennie sent. He added that his wife enjoyed it over some "Green Brothers corn meal batter cakes."

Jenny Lind Bread

1 quart sifted flour
A lump of butter the size of an egg
2 teacups milk
4 eggs
1½ teaspoonfuls soda
2 teaspoonfuls cream of tartar

Bake twenty minutes in a quick oven.

Cream Biscuit

1 quart sifted flour
4 teaspoonfuls cream of tartar
2 teaspoonfuls fine table salt
2 ounces fresh, good butter
2 even teaspoonfuls soda
1 pint pure, sweet cream

Combine the flour, cream of tartar and salt so that both the latter are well diffused through the flour. Add the butter and mix well. Dissolve the soda in the cream and add it to the flour mixture. The dough ought to be very soft; but should it be too soft, add a little more flour. Work it well, roll it out half an inch thick, cut with a biscuit cutter and bake in a quick oven five minutes.

Date and Bacon Muffins

¼ cupful butter
2 tablespoonfuls sugar
1 egg
½ teaspoonful salt
2 cupfuls flour
5 teaspoonfuls baking powder
1 cupful milk
4 long strips crisp bacon, broken in pieces
¾ cupful diced dates

Cream butter; add sugar and egg and beat thoroughly. Sift salt, flour, and baking powder together and add to first mixture alternately with milk. Fold in bacon and dates and place in buttered muffin pans, filling about ⅔ full. Bake in a moderate oven for about 25 minutes.

Corn Biscuits

1⅜ cupfuls general-purpose flour
⅝ cupful cornmeal
2 tablespoonfuls sugar
2 teaspoonfuls any baking powder
½ teaspoonful salt
1 egg
¾ cupful sour cream
½ teaspoonful soda

Sift the flour, cornmeal, sugar, baking powder, and salt together. Beat the egg, add the sour cream, in which the soda has been dissolved, and add all at one time to the dry ingredients. Stir only until mixed. Turn onto a floured surface and knead lightly. Pat out to ¾-inch thickness, cut into rounds, and place in a greased pan. Bake in a hot oven (450°) for 15 minutes. Serve piping hot.

A Sally Lunn

This cake is named after the inventress.

1½ pounds flour
2 ounces butter, warmed
1 pint milk
1 salt-spoonful of salt
3 eggs, well beaten
2 tablespoons of the best fresh yeast

Sift flour into a pan and make a hole in the middle; combine butter, milk, salt, eggs, and yeast. Pour liquid into hole, mix the flour well into the other ingredients, and put the whole into a square tin pan that has been greased with butter. Cover it and set it in a warm place; when it is quite light, bake it in a moderate oven. Send it to table hot, and eat it with butter. Or you may bake it on a griddle in small rings, pulling the cakes open and buttering them when brought to table.

Cakes

Some Cake-Making Tips

* Use none but the best family flour.
* The butter used for cake-making should be fresh.
* Do not attempt to make cake without fresh eggs, which when placed in water will sink to the bottom.
* The whites of eggs must always be added last.
* For baking cakes, the best guide is practice and experience, so much depending on the state of the fire that it is impossible to lay down any infallible rules.
* All baking pans should be well greased and then filled but little more than half.
* Immediately after taking a cake from the oven, it should be inverted on a cake cooler and the pan removed. If the cake cools in the pan it tends to become sticky.
* It is a good plan to let the flour air and sun several hours before using it; as this makes it much lighter.
* In summer, always try to make the cake before breakfast, or as early in the morning as possible.
* Never use pulverized sugar as it is apt to have plaster of Paris or other foreign elements in it.
* Neither the butter and sugar nor the eggs should be beaten in a tin vessel, as the coldness of the vessel will prevent them from becoming light.
* In damp weather it is sometimes difficult to beat the white of egg to a stiff froth.
* Every housekeeper should have a closed cake-box in which to put fruit cake after cooking it and wrapping it in a thick napkin.

Gingerbread Fit for the King

¾ cup brown sugar
¾ cup butter
¾ cup molasses
2 eggs, beaten light
2½ cups flour
1 teaspoon ginger, powdered
1 teaspoon clove, powdered
1 teaspoon cinnamon, powdered
2 teaspoons soda
1 cup boiling water

Cream butter and sugar and add molasses and eggs. Sift together flour and spices; add to the molasses mixture. Dissolve soda in boiling water and add to the rest; blend well. Bake in a long greased tin in a moderate oven for about 40 minutes.

Note: Serve warm with a hot lemon sauce! (page 87)

Butter Sponge Cake with Lemon Sauce

14 eggs
The weight of 14 eggs in sugar
The weight of 8 eggs in flour
The weight of 6 eggs in butter
Grated rind of 1 lemon
Juice of 2 lemons

Bake quickly and serve with a lemon sauce.

Note: Nine different recipes for sponge cake appear in the *Housekeeping in Old Virginia* cookbook, and most use the weight of eggs to determine the amount of the other ingredients. (See tables for egg weights.) One recipe calls for powdered sugar; another that calls for 14 eggs requires one pound of sugar. Still another suggests, "A large cake will require fully an hour for baking." Tattered edges and much discoloration characterize the pages holding these sponge cake and the adjoining jelly cake recipes.

Lemon Sauce

1 pound sugar
3 ounces butter
½ teacup water
Juice and sliced rinds of 2 lemons
2 eggs, separated

Pour all except the eggs into a saucepan, and while it is coming to a boil, beat the egg yolks and add them. When well boiled, take mixture from the fire and add the egg whites, beaten to a stiff froth. To be eaten hot with sponge cake.

California Upside-Down Fruit Cake

1 cupful brown sugar
4 tablespoonfuls butter
8 slices pineapple
8 maraschino cherries

Batter

1½ cupfuls sugar
½ cupful shortening
2 beaten eggs
¾ cupful sour milk
1 teaspoonful soda
2 cupfuls cake flour
½ teaspoonful cinnamon
¼ teaspoonful cloves
¼ teaspoonful allspice
½ cupful chopped raisins
½ cupful chopped nutmeats

Spread the brown sugar evenly in the bottom of a long narrow baking pan. Dot with the butter and arrange pineapple slices over this mixture. Place a cherry in the center of each pineapple slice. Cream the sugar and shortening together. Add the beaten eggs and mix well. Add the milk in which the soda has been dissolved, then the flour sifted with the spices. Fold in the raisins and nutmeats, dusted with flour, and pour over the pineapple mixture, spreading evenly. Bake in a moderate oven for 45 minutes. Turn out upside down. Serve warm.

Note: A 9x11-inch pan works well for this rich and spicy, dressed-up cousin of the pineapple upside-down cake.

Green Mansion

Pineapple Upside-Down Cake

⅓ cup butter, melted
1 cup white sugar
1 egg, well beaten
1 teaspoon orange extract
1¾ cup flour
3 teaspoons baking powder
¼ teaspoon salt
½ cup milk
3 tablespoons butter
¾ cup brown sugar
5 or 6 slices canned pineapple

Cream the butter and sugar together; add the egg and flavoring. Sift together dry ingredients and add to the first mixture alternately with the milk. Cream together the butter and brown sugar. Rub the bottom and sides of a heavy frying pan (one that can be put safely into the oven) with the brown sugar mixture and place the pineapple slices evenly over it. Pour batter over all and bake at 375° until lightly browned. Immediately invert onto waiting platter. Serve hot or warm.

The original recipe, from what appears to be a maga-ine or a label, shows great use and much deterioration. Miss Jennie copied the recipe onto a file box card, ut wrote only the list of ingredients. The card, too, ears its share of spatter marks. On her card copy Jennie noted that three teaspoons baking powder was oo much." As a result, you also might want to djust the amount.

Nut Cake

2 cups sugar
½ cup butter
4 whole eggs, beaten
3 cups all-purpose flour
2 teaspoons baking powder
1 cup milk
2 cups hickory nuts
1 teaspoon vanilla

Cream sugar and butter; add eggs. Sift together flour and baking powder and add alternately with milk to butter mixture. Add nuts and vanilla. Bake in a moderate oven.

Note: This recipe is one of only four handwritten in the "Manuscript Receipts" section at the back of *Housekeeping in Old Virginia* and then recopied, indicating its long-favored status in the Green dining room.

Hickory nut Cake

10 eggs

115 WEST ORMSBY AVENUE
LOUISVILLE, KY.

1 lb. flour (brown flour.)

1 lb. butter

1½ lbs. raisins

1 lb. sugar

1 lb. hickory nuts as nearly whole

½ tumbler brandy

½ lb. citron

1 nut meg

heaping tea spoon of cream of ta

1 even tea spoon soda

Bake 4 hours in slow o

Hickory Nut Cake

10 eggs
1 pound flour (brown flour)
1 pound butter
1½ pounds raisins
1 pound sugar
1 pound hickory nuts (as nearly whole as possible)
½ tumbler brandy
½ pound citron
1 nutmeg, grated
1 heaping teaspoon cream of tartar
1 even teaspoon soda

Bake four hours in a slow oven.

On October 10, 1898, nineteen-year-old Jennie wrote her younger brother at Centre College in Danville, Kentucky, that she and older brother Willis had been to hunt hickory nuts but found only a few. She added that chestnuts were coming in and she would send him some.

Blackberry Jam Cake

1½ c. of butter
2 " " sugar
4 " " flour
2 " " jam
6 eggs beat separately
2 teaspoonful of soda dissolved
in 6 tablespoonful of buttermilk
2 teasp. " of cinnamon
2 " " cloves
2 " " spice
2 " " nutmeg
a cup of raisins may be
added if desired.

Blackberry Jam Cake

1½ cups butter
2 cups sugar
6 eggs, beaten
2 teaspoons soda
6 tablespoons buttermilk
4 cups flour
2 cups blackberry jam
2 teaspoons cinnamon
2 teaspoons cloves
2 teaspoons allspice
2 teaspoons nutmeg
1 cups raisins (if desired)

Cream butter and sugar and add eggs. Dissolve soda in buttermilk and add alternately with flour to sugar mixture. Mix in jam, spices, and raisins. Bake in greased and floured cake pans at 350° until done. Allow to cool for 5-10 minutes and remove from baking pans.

Merry Christmas Cake

2 cups flour
2 teaspoonfuls baking powder
1 cup cornstarch
1 cup butter
2 cups sugar
½ cup sweet milk
Whites of 8 eggs, beaten very stiff

Combine flour, baking powder, cornstarch. Cream butter and sugar together, and add flour mixture alternately with milk. Gently fold in beaten egg whites. Bake in jelly-cake pans. When cold, spread tops and sides with an icing made of the whites of three additional eggs and one pound of sugar. Grate fresh cocoanut over each layer of icing.

Around Christmas time in 1885, Jennie's mother wrote her own mother of her fond memories of Christmas when she was a child. She then described her children as noisy and laughing merrily as they assembled "to do justice to the Santa Claus cake and candy." Jennie was barely six years old at the time, and her brothers were 15, 8, and 3.

Ann Eliza Robertson's White Fruit Cake

2½ cups flour
2 teaspoons baking powder
2 cups sugar
1 cup butter
1 cup milk
Whites of 7 eggs
1 pound each: white raisins, figs, and almonds
¼ pound citron
Candied cherries, pineapple, orange and lemon peels, other nuts of choice

Dec. 16, 51, Bart Brown, st officer of itizens Fidelity Bank of Louisville, wrote to thank Jennie for the Christmas presents, delicious cake and a country ham.

Note: The Green collection contains three copies of this recipe, the oldest in a letter from Miss Robertson. The recipe is in one of Miss Jennie's personalized envelopes with the following on the front in her handwriting: "Ann Eliza Robertson's white fruit cake receipt enclosed in a letter written about 1912." Two other copies are in Miss Jennie's handwriting, with one recipe adding the candied fruit and nuts. None, however, include mixing or baking instructions.

Ann Eliza Robertson was a dicated correspondent, sending Jennie numerous post-rds, letters, and birthday wishes throughout the ears. Ann Eliza lived in Elizabethtown, Kentucky, proximately thirty-five miles from Falls of Rough.

Fruit Cake - Mrs. Ho.

3 1/2 lbs seeded raisins
1 1/2 lb citron
2 " currants. clean & dry in cloth rubbing
1 lb figs
1 lb almonds
1 " English walnuts & pecans
Flour all well from the batter - & mix well -
1 lb butter creamed well
1 lb sugar together -
12 eggs beat separately -
1 lb flour
1 teacup of brandy or whiskey
1 tbl - salt - 1 tbl ginger - 2 nutmeg
dissolve 1 teasp - soda in 1 tbl
water beat with 1 cup molasses
juice one orange and
one lemon -

Mrs. Glove's * Fruit Cake

3½ pounds seeded raisins
1½ pounds citron
2 pounds currants
1 pound figs, cut up
1 pound almonds, chopped
1 pound English walnuts or pecans, chopped
1 pound butter
1 pound sugar
12 eggs, beaten separately
1 pound flour
1 teacup brandy or whiskey
1 tablespoon cinnamon
1 tablespoon ginger
2 grated nutmegs
1 teaspoon soda
1 tablespoon water
1 cup molasses
Juice of one orange
Juice of one lemon

Note: This recipe contains only partial instructions, the legible portions being as follows: Steam raisins, citron, and currants 2 minutes and then put in a dry cloth overnight to dry. Flour the figs, almonds, and walnuts well before putting them in the batter. Cream butter and sugar together well. Dissolve soda in the tablespoon of water and mix with molasses, to which has been added the citrus juices.

A similar fruit cake recipe from the collection provides further instructions: To the butter mixture add the spices and beaten egg yolks, alternating with the beaten whites. Next add the flour, fruit, and nuts, and then stir in the molasses mixture. Lastly, add the brandy. Stir to blend all ingredients. Pour into a well-buttered and floured tube or loaf cake pan. Bake in a moderate oven until done.

*This same recipe, handwritten in the "Manuscript Receipts" section of *Housekeeping in Old Virginia*, is attributed not to Mrs. Glove, but to Mrs. J. J. McHenry.

Devil's Food Cake

1 cup brown sugar
1 cup grated chocolate
½ cup milk
3 egg yolks
½ cup butter, softened
1 cup brown sugar
½ cup sour milk
2½ cups flour
2 scant teaspoons soda

Mix brown sugar and chocolate; add milk. Heat to dissolve sugar and chocolate. Allow to cool while mixing together remaining ingredients; then add chocolate mixture. Bake in a slow oven and out will come food fit for the Devil.

In a June 4, 1940, letter a Louisville friend wrote Jennie that her husband said the cake they had Sunday (one Jennie had sent them) "was the best he ever ate."

Rolled Jelly Cake

3 eggs, separated
1 teacup sugar
1 teacup flour

Beat the yolks of the eggs till light, then add the sugar; continue beating for some time, then add the whites beaten to a stiff froth. Next put in the flour, a little at a time. Bake in a long pan, well greased; when done turn out on a bread board, then cover the top with jelly and roll while warm, and slice as needed.

Note: This recipe occupies a well-spattered page and appears to be marked as a favorite.

Chess Cake

1 pound butter
1 pound sugar
3½ cups flour
1 pound seedless raisins
1 pound currants
¼ pound citron, cut fine
1 dozen French candied dates, chopped
Yolks of 28 eggs
1 dozen French candies, cut up
1 teaspoon cinnamon
1 teaspoon nutmeg
1 teaspoon cloves
1 glass whiskey

Cream butter and sugar. Mix flour with all fruits until they are well coated. Combine with sugar mixture and add egg yolks and remaining ingredients. Make a plain white cake and alternate a fruit layer, putting a white icing in between. (¼ recipe makes a good size cake)

White Cake

1 cup butter
3 cups sugar
3 cups flour
3 teaspoonfuls cream of tartar
1 teaspoonful soda
1 cup sweet milk
Whites of 5 eggs

Cream butter and sugar; sift flour with cream of tartar and soda. Add flour mixture alternately with milk to butter mixture. Mix well. Beat egg whites till stiff and fold into batter. Bake in moderate oven.

Cookies & Small Cakes

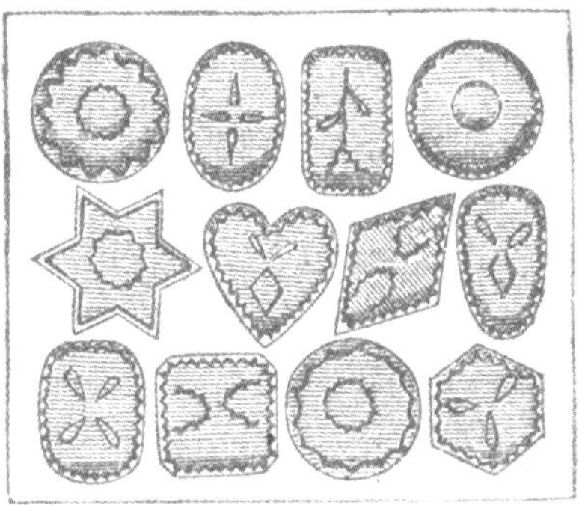

Pecan Cakes with Boiled Frosting

2 eggs, beaten
1 cup brown sugar
5/8 cup flour
1/3 teaspoon salt
1/4 teaspoon baking powder
1 cup chopped pecans

Mix eggs and sugar and blend thoroughly. Sift together flour, salt, and baking powder; add gradually to sugar and egg mixture. When batter is smooth, add pecans. Pour into very small muffin pans and bake at 350° about 20 minutes. If desired, cover with boiled frosting.

Boiled Frosting

1 cup granulated sugar
⅓ cup hot water
1 large egg white
⅛ teaspoon cream of tartar
1 teaspoon flavoring extract

Boil sugar and water until it threads. Meanwhile, combine egg white and cream of tartar and beat stiff. Pour syrup slowly into egg white mixture, beating constantly until thick enough to spread. Add flavoring and cover cakes while warm.

Note: This frosting recipe has a penciled *X* before it, an indication that Miss Jennie marked it for use. She also used this method of indicating a selection in other subjects: exhibit entries to see, paintings to order, books to read, excursions to take, etc.

NAPLES, FLORIDA

Pecan Sticks

2 cups sifted flour
1 cup chopped pecans
4 tablespoons confectioner's sugar
2 tablespoons vanilla
3/4 cup butter (or margarine)

Sift flour & sugar together, work in butter as for pastry, add nuts & vanilla.

Roll a piece of dough (size of English walnut) into "finger". Bake on ungreased baking sheet at 325° until delicately brown –
Roll in confec. sugar while still a little warm.

Pecan Sticks

2 cups sifted flour
4 tablespoons confectioner's sugar
¾ cup butter (or margarine)
1 cup chopped pecans
2 tablespoons vanilla

Sift flour and sugar together. Work in butter as for pastry. Add nuts and vanilla. Roll a piece of dough the size of an English walnut into a "finger." Bake on ungreased baking sheet at 325° until delicately brown. Roll in confectioner's sugar while still a little warm.

In 1937, while wintering in Naples, Florida, Miss Jennie and her brother Willis participated in a masquerade ball. The evening's festivities, announced as the "Follies of 1937," consisted of a grand march of masqueraded guests followed by talent performances. One guest recited the poem "Casey at the Bat" and another danced the hula. No evidence suggests the brother and sister dressed in masquerade, but Willis served as one of the judges, and Jennie was a member of the arrangement committee.

Folded Fruit Cakes

3½ cups cake flour
¼ teaspoon soda
¼ teaspoon salt
¾ cup shortening
1 cup sugar
¾ cup evaporated milk
¼ cup water

Mix flour, soda, and salt. Cream together shortening and sugar. Add flour mixture to sugar mixture alternately with milk diluted with ¼ cup water. Mix well after each addition. Turn out on floured board; roll ⅛ inch thick and cut into 3-inch rounds. Put on half of each round 1 teaspoon fruit filling; fold and cover with other half of round. Pinch edges together with fork. Put in greased baking pan and sprinkle sugar over top. Bake in moderate oven until brown. Yields 5 dozen cakes.

Filling

¾ cup sugar
¾ cup evaporated milk
¼ cup water

¼ cup pitted dates, finely chopped
¼ cup figs, finely chopped
¼ cup raisins, chopped
½ cup nuts, chopped

Mix sugar, milk, and water; heat until sugar is dissolved. Stir in fruits and continue cooking until mixture is thick. Cool and then add nuts.

Orange Tea Biscuits

2 cups of flour
5 teaspoons baking powder
1 teaspoon salt
5 tablespoons lard
About ¾ cup milk
Orange marmalade

Sift dry ingredients together and work the lard in with a fork. Add only enough milk to make the mixture the right consistency to roll. Roll thin and cut out rounds with a biscuit cutter. Spread half the rounds with marmalade; cover with rest of rounds. Press together; brush with milk and bake ten minutes in hot oven.

Honey Cakes

2 ounces butter, melted
1 cup honey
Rind of one large lemon, grated
1 tablespoon fresh lemon juice
2 ounces almonds, cut fine
¼ teaspoon mace
½ teaspoon soda
2½ cups flour
1 cup sugar
½ cup water

Mix all ingredients thoroughly; cover and set in a cool place until the next morning. Roll in sheets ½ inch thick and cut in squares; place in greased and floured pans and bake 15 to 20 minutes in a moderate oven. Meanwhile, boil to thread the sugar and water. When cakes are baked, wash them with slightly cooled sirup.

Note: Mace is a fragrant and highly aromatic spice consisting of the dried external fibrous covering of the nutmeg.

Delicate Tea Cakes

Whites of 3 eggs, beaten to a froth
1 cupful pulverized sugar
½ cupful sweet milk
2½ cupfuls flour
1 teaspoon cream of tartar
½ teaspoonful soda
½ cupful melted butter
1 teaspoonful almonds, chopped

Combine egg whites, sugar, and milk. Sift together flour, cream of tartar, and soda. Combine the two mixtures and mix well. Add butter and almonds and pour into small cake molds. Bake in a moderate oven until browned around the edges.

Ice Box Cookies

1½ cups melted shortening (Crisco)
1 cup white sugar
1 cup brown sugar
3 eggs
1 teaspoon each: salt, cinnamon, soda
1 cup nuts, chopped
4 cups flour

Mix all ingredients and roll into two long rolls. Wrap in waxed paper and refrigerate until well chilled. Slice thinly and bake in a hot oven till lightly browned.

Cocoanut Macaroons

1½ cups powdered sugar
Cream
2 egg whites, beaten very stiff
2 cups grated cocoanut

Combine just enough cream to dampen the sugar well. Gradually whip into the beaten egg whites the moistened sugar, and then beat in the cocoanut. When the mixture is light, drop it by the teaspoonful upon buttered parchment paper and bake very quickly to a very light brown.

Bop

3 eggs, beaten
4 tablespoonfuls flour
1 pint milk
1 tablespoonful butter
Mixture of butter, sugar, and nutmeg to taste

Add flour and milk to eggs, and put the mixture in three prepared pans of the same size. Dot the butter on top in small pieces and bake in a quick oven. While hot, pile on top of each other with a mixture of butter, sugar, and nutmeg between. Serve with any pudding sauce or with cream. Crushed strawberries are a delightful addition.

In a letter dated June 6, 1931, a friend referred to a recent visit at Miss Jennie's when she took home some strawberry plants. She also speculated that Jennie's flower garden by the time of the letter must have been in full bloom and beautiful.

Fluffy Ruffles

1 egg, beaten
½ cup sugar
2 teaspoons cooking oil
¾ cup rolled oats
⅓ teaspoon salt
⅓ teaspoon vanilla

Mix all ingredients and drop onto an oiled baking tin. Bake in a moderate oven until brown.

Ginger Snaps

One-half cupful of butter, one cupful each of sugar and molasses, one teaspoonful of ginger, two teaspoonfuls of baking powder, and flour enough to make stiff to roll. Mix all, roll, cut out, and bake in a moderate oven.

Lady Fingers

⅔ cup flour
Dash of salt
4 egg yolks, beaten thick
6 egg whites, beaten very stiff
⅔ cup powdered sugar

Sift together flour and salt twice; then add egg yolks and beat thoroughly. Combine egg whites with sugar and fold into yolk mixture. Press from a pastry tube onto buttered or waxed paper in long, narrow fingers. Dust with powdered sugar and bake 8 minutes in a slow oven.

Jennie Scott Green was born on September 26, 1879, to Ella and Lafayette Green, who had married almost thirteen years earlier in 1866. Her father's uncle, Willis Green, and his wife had taken in Lafayette and his three orphaned siblings in the mid-1840s. When Willis Green died in 1862, he left the entire estate, including the business enterprises at Falls of Rough, to Lafayette.

Willis Green founded the remote Kentucky village in the 1830s around a water-powered milling business on a small falls of the Rough River. By the time of his death, those businesses had grown to include a sawmill, gristmill, wool-carding mill, general store, and large farming operation. By the turn of the century, a hotel, bank, train depot, school, Methodist church, and parsonage also helped serve the community of approximately 250 inhabitants, most of whom worked for the Greens and lived in the tenant houses they built. The Greens, in fact, owned the whole town.

Jennie's mother, the former Rebecca Eleanor "Ella" Scott of Frankfort, Kentucky, most likely met Jennie's father, Lafayette Green, as a result of acquaintances he made while serving as a congressman in that capital city in 1859-60. Their formal courtship did not begin until the winter of 1864-65, when Ella was twenty-three and Lafayette twenty-nine. Ella had grown up in Frankfort and was accustomed to the aristocratic lifestyle of her parents, relatives of Kentucky's renowned Breckinridges and Browns. It was her mother's aristocratic background that would determine young Jennie's upbringing and the adult Jennie would become.

Jennie at age two

1950s

Jennie (middle), early 1900s

Jennie in her 30's

Jennie in her 20's

Around 1920

Jennie in her 40's

Green General Store "Main Street," Falls of Rough, KY 1940s

Letters from her mother and other relatives reveal that Jennie was a spoiled child. An older sister, born in 1868, lived only one year; another older sister was stillborn. So when Jennie came into the family after the birth of two sons, her father, especially, doted upon her. Once, when her mother threatened to slap the three-and-a-half year-old if she didn't behave, little Jennie responded, "Now Momma you wouldn't hit Papa's darling pet daughter when shes[*sic*] sick." Shortly before her third birthday Jennie acquired a baby brother, who eventually stole away some of her father's attention.

Ella was adamant that all her children receive the best of training. To help accomplish her goal, she exposed Jennie and her brothers to religious activities at the Methodist church that she helped to organize, build (on Green property), and support. In addition, the house was full of books, and Mrs. Green frequently read to her children until she was hoarse. Their mother held high hopes for all four of her offspring and hired teachers, who usually lived with the family, to see that they became well schooled.

Although hard work and good behavior were important, Mrs. Green recognized the role of play and good times for the children. She indulged them, especially during summer vacations when friends or relatives arrived, often for extensive visits. On one occasion when Jennie's youngest brother took a huge bullfrog into the parlor, their mother only remarked that her head swam "after looking at such an ugly beast." At another time, when Jennie was only four years old, her mother wrote that pandemonium had let loose in the sitting room, where eight children of "all sizes, colors and ages" were "kicking up the dust" as they prepared for a tea party. Mrs. Green, in fact, held a reputation as a fun-loving organizer of pageants, parties, and other social events. Not surprising, then, is the fact that children and, as her own grew, young people tended to "collect" at the Green home at Falls of Rough. As a result, Jennie grew up accustomed to frequent entertainment and the company of playmates and friends of her own social class.

Jennie and her brothers also witnessed the generosity and compassion of their mother who, although she frequently referred to the area's inhabitants as uneducated heathens, sent clothes to those in need and served as community nursemaid during epidemics. Their father, likewise, was a hard worker who often indulged his children, especially his daughter. The four siblings, therefore, developed under the nurturing umbrella of parents who provided the best of examples.

Letters indicate that Jennie attended home school and then, just before her fifteenth birthday in 1894, entered the Princeton Collegiate Institute in Princeton, Kentucky. She was frequently away from home as a young teenager, so the possibility exists that she had also attended classes in Louisville or Frankfort, where she often visited with family or friends. Like her mother, Jennie enjoyed playing the piano, which she did quite well. At Princeton Collegiate Institute she studied rhetoric, algebra, history, French, physics, drawing, music, Bible, and Latin, at which she excelled.

While at Princeton, Jennie easily became a part of the school's social whirl. According to one source, soon after her arrival Jennie was the most popular girl there. Although at first she showed little interest in boys, by her second month at the Institute she became a part of a budding love affair with a Princeton native son, Shelly Ransford Smith. Their love letters, typical expressions of youthful infatuation, continued for the next three years. Even though the love affair then faded and Smith married and had a family, they continued to correspond until at least 1933.

Jennie did not enroll in the 1895 fall term at Princeton, probably due to the ill health of her mother. After her mother's death from "cancer and Bright's disease" in March 1896, Jennie spent some parts of the next year and a half either at home or in Louisville, where she might have attended boarding school. She then returned to Princeton for the 1897 spring semester, hoping especially to pursue her study of music. At the close of that semester, however, she ended her formal education and returned to Falls of Rough, where she began to assume duties as mistress of the household. By this time her two older brothers had returned home after attending Centre College in Danville, Kentucky, to become partners in their father's businesses.

Correspondence indicates that except for some time spent in Louisville during the winter of 1897-98, Jennie returned permanently to her home at Falls of Rough in mid-1897. She occasionally escaped to visit family and friends in distant cities and, in fact, was in Atlanta, Georgia, when her father died of a heart attack in 1907. She was awaiting his arrival there for their shared journey to Florida, their typical winter retreat.

In 1909 Jennie made her first trip to Europe, where she toured for three months. Her second trip followed in late 1911, just after, for unexplained reasons, she sold her one-fourth interest in the family's businesses and properties to her brothers for "one dollar and other valuable considerations." She returned in April of 1912 and enjoyed recounting how she had viewed the notorious iceberg but escaped the fate of those on the *Titanic* by being on a smaller and slower boat, just hours ahead of the famous "unsinkable" ship.

Over the next thirty-three years Jennie ran the household, but under the auspices of her brothers, for they controlled all the finances. She and brother Willis traveled annually to Naples, Florida, where they spent the winter months, and to the eastern United States in the summer. She traveled to Louisville to enjoy the opera and ballet and frequently entertained friends and family at home. She also spent much time reading and growing flowers, especially roses.

In the early 1940s her three brothers, now in their early sixties and seventies, began to develop health problems. By May 1945 Jennie was the sole survivor and the last of the Greens of Falls of Rough, for neither she nor her brothers had ever married. She was also now in charge of the Falls of Rough businesses: a gristmill, a large farming operation, and a general store. Despite her inexperience and the general decline in profits, Jennie insisted upon maintaining operations, even though the stress of all her new responsibilities, combined with the emotional strain resulting from her brothers' deaths, began to affect her health. However, she continued to spend July and August in cooler climates and, in some years, parts of January and February in warmer climates. Due to health problems, by 1953 she had installed an electric lift chair on her back stairs to aid her descent from her bedroom, and for a while she used a wheelchair. But she eventually progressed beyond its use and, as late as 1962, spent another summer in Wequetonsing, Michigan, a favorite vacationing destination.

Because she had no direct heirs, Jennie spent the last several years of her life searching for a relative willing to move, upon her death, to her beloved home place. In the late 1950s she chose a distant maternal cousin, Mary Perry McGee of Houston, Texas, as heir. About that same time Jennie donated many of the older family manuscripts to Louisville's Filson Club; however, many documents remained in the twenty-two-room manor house. In the late 1960s Mary McGee donated thousands more letters to the Kentucky Library in Bowling Green, Kentucky, and yet more papers hid in the many shelves, drawers, and bookcases of the home. The pantry cabinets, too, stored their share of treasures.

Jennie Scott Green died just before her eighty-sixth birthday on September 5, 1965, due primarily to health complications of her advancing age. For the first time in over 125 years, there was no Green to rule the kitchen at Falls of Rough. However, Miss Jennie, as she was known, left her legacy: a beautiful country home filled with her family's rich history.

Pies & Fillings

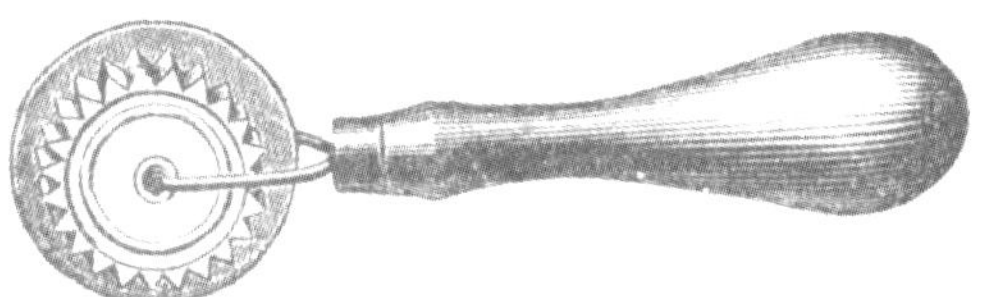

Miss Jennie's Dining Room

Hints for Making Pastry

All utensils and materials should be very cold. A marble slab, a glass rolling pin, and hands as clean as those of a modern surgeon are necessities. Successful pastry can only be made with clean, cold utensils and dainty fingers.

"Cannot Fail" Pie Crust

2 tablespoons shortening
1 cup flour
Pinch salt
3 tablespoons cold water

Mix all with fork and roll on a lightly floured surface. Line pan and fill as desired or, if a pre-baked crust is desired, prick bottom and sides and bake in a hot oven for 10 to 12 minutes, or till lightly browned. Allow to cool before adding filling. Makes a single crust.

Plain Paste

3 cups sifted pastry flour
1 teaspoon salt
1 cup lard
Ice water
2 tablespoons butter

Combine flour, salt, and lard; chop with knife until in small crumbs. Put in ice-box for several hours, and then add enough ice water to make a soft dough. Roll out, spread with butter, and roll again. Place on ice until ready to use. This will yield two crusts.

Molasses Pie

Yolks of four eggs (reserve whites)
1 cup sugar
1 cup molasses
Butter the size of an egg
1 tablespoon flour

Beat egg yolks and mix with remaining ingredients. Fill two unbaked pie crusts with the mixture and, when baked, cover with the egg whites well beaten with a little sugar. Brown lightly either under the broiler (Watch closely!) or in a slow oven.

Graham Cracker Pie Shell

1 ½ cups graham cracker crumbs
⅓ cup powdered sugar
½ cup (scant) butter

Mix all ingredients and press into pie pan. Place in refrigerator or cold place and allow to stand for several hours. Then put in pie filling to serve.

Note: This recipe, from Miss Jennie's recipe box, wears lots of stains, evidence that it likely was a favorite. Perhaps it was produced from her kitchen even before she owned a refrigerator, as the directions offer an alternative.

Lemon Chiffon Pie

1 envelope unflavored gelatin
¼ cup cold water
4 eggs, separated
1 cup sugar, divided
½ cup lemon juice, freshly squeezed
½ teaspoon salt
1 teaspoon lemon rind, grated

Soften gelatin in water and set aside. Beat egg yolks and add ½ cup sugar, lemon juice, and salt. Cook in double boiler until of custard consistency, stirring constantly. Stir gelatin mixture and add to hot custard; blend well. Add lemon rind; cool. Beat egg whites with remaining ½ cup sugar till stiff. When custard begins to thicken, remove from heat and fold in egg whites. Fill baked pie shell or graham cracker crust; chill. If desired, top with whipped cream just before serving.

Caramel Pie

1 cup sugar, divided
2 generous tablespoonfuls flour
2 eggs, separated and yolks well beaten
¾ pint sweet milk
1 tablespoon melted butter
Vanilla to taste
1 baked piecrust, cooled
2 egg whites
¼ cup sugar

Mix ½ cup of sugar with the flour; stir in egg yolks and blend. Gradually add sweet milk, stirring continually until smooth. Brown remaining ½ cup of sugar in a heavy skillet by heating over a slow fire and shaking the pan occasionally; do not stir. When sugar is brown, slowly add the milk mixture to the skillet, stirring continually over a slow fire. Stir and cook until thick and then take from the fire. Add vanilla and melted butter and pour into crust. When cooled somewhat, drop on top of the filling spoonfuls of the whites that have been whipped light with the ¼ cup sugar; brown lightly. The effect is pretty.

Mince meat -

A round of beef or a lean piece
of shoulder is best -
Suet from around a kidney
Chop fine together after
meat is cooked -
3 lb of apples sliced thin
chopped fine & mixed with m
3/4 lb citron shredded
3 lb currants
1 lb seedless raisins
2 lb stoned malaga raisins
1 lb powdered sugar
1/4 oz cloves 1 cin - 1/2 of ma
1/2 nutmeg - tbl of allspice -
1 teasp of salt
1 pt French brandy
Stir thoroughly - put on fire and
heat just to boiling point
Put in cool place near [illegible]
and let stand few weeks
Add candied orange peel

Mrs. Gladstone's Mincemeat

A round of beef or a lean piece of shoulder is best
Suet from around a kidney
3 pounds of apples, sliced thin and chopped fine
¾ pounds citron, shredded
3 pounds currants
1 pound seedless raisins
2 pounds sliced Malaya raisins
1 pound powdered sugar
¼ ounce each cloves and cinnamon
½ ounce each mace and nutmeg
1 tablespoon allspice
1 teaspoon salt
1 pint French brandy
Candied orange peel (to taste)

After meat is cooked, chop finely together with suet; add apples. Mix in all other ingredients except orange peel, stirring thoroughly; put on fire and heat just to boiling. Put in cold place and let stand five weeks. Add orange peel. Note: Due to age, use, and Jennie's writing, this recipe is barely legible in the "Manuscript Receipts" section of *Housekeeping in Old Virginia*. Jennie recopied the recipe in a more legible form, but omitted Mrs. Gladstone's name.

Apple Pie with Whipped Cream

6 tart apples
2 tablespoons sugar
1 teaspoon butter, in bits
½ teaspoon cinnamon or dash of nutmeg and cloves
1 cup whipped cream

Line pie tin with plain paste and fill with peeled, cored, and halved apples. Combine sugar, butter, and spice(s) and sprinkle over apples. Bake until apples are soft; cover with whipped cream just before serving.

Raisin Pie

1½ cups seeded raisins, chopped
1 cup cold water
½ cup sugar
1 lemon, cut in thin slices
1 tablespoon flour
1 double paste, unbaked

Line a pie-tin with paste. Mix raisins, water, and sugar and pour into the lined pan. Combine lemon slices with flour and spread over the raisin mixture. Cover with strips of paste and bake.

Orange Cream Pie

1 cup water
½ cup sugar
Small piece of butter
¼ cup cornstarch
2 eggs, separated
Juice and grated rind of a large orange
1 tablespoon sugar
Pinch of baking powder
1 lightly baked piecrust, cooled

Combine water, sugar, and butter in a saucepan. Boil together and add cornstarch which has been rubbed smooth in a little cold water. Continue to boil, stirring all the time, for one minute. Remove from fire. Meanwhile, beat the egg yolks and add orange juice and rind; add to the cooled filling and pour all into the baked crust. Combine the egg whites, sugar, and baking powder and beat till stiff. Spread over cooked pie and leave in the oven just long enough to brown the meringue lightly.

Jennie's family enjoy citrus fruits unavailable to the average family. maternal grandparents owned a winter home in Flor and frequently mailed the Greens the products of th groves. Because the fruits did not keep well, Jenni mother likely sought recipes using them. Jennie continued to vacation in Florida long after her grandparents' and parents' deaths, and her files contain man recipes featuring oranges and lemons.

Dessert Puddings & Sauces

Mrs. Glove's Plum Pudding

1½ pounds raisins
1 pound currants
⅜ pound citron
1 pound figs
1 pound dates
¾ pound shelled almonds
1 cup molasses
1 teaspoon soda
1 teaspoon cream of tartar
Peel of 5 lemons and 5 oranges
1 tablespoon cinnamon
1 nutmeg, grated
1 pint sherry wine
1 tumbler brandy or whiskey
1 quart cherry or strawberry preserves
1 pint stale breadcrumbs
1 pound chopped beef suet
6 eggs, both white and yellow
¾ pound sugar
½ pint flour
½ tablespoon ground cloves

Chop fruit and nuts. Dissolve soda in molasses and add the cream of tartar. Mix all ingredients together and fill prepared molds. Steam from 5 to 6 hours. This recipe will yield six melon-shape puddings.

A Baked Bread Pudding

Take a stale five cent loaf of bread; cut off all the crust, and grate or rub the crumb as fine as possible. Boil a quart of rich milk, and pour it hot over the bread; then stir in a quarter of a pound of butter, and the same quantity of sugar, a glass of wine and brandy mixed, or a glass of rose water. Or you may omit the liquor and substitute the grated peel of a large lemon. Add a tablespoonful of mixed cinnamon and nutmeg powdered. Stir the whole very well, cover it, and set it away for half an hour. Then let it cool. Beat seven or eight eggs very light, and stir them gradually into the mixture after it is cold. Then butter a deep dish, and bake the pudding an hour. Send it to the table cool.

Note: This recipe, from the 1842 edition of *Directions for Cooking*, is a contribution from Ann Green's kitchen. The book opens easily to this page, which holds another bread pudding recipe and wears many spatter stains.

Ginger Pudding with Orange Sauce

½ teaspoons soda
1½ teaspoons ginger
½ teaspoon salt
1⅝ cups entire wheat flour
½ cup molasses
1½ tablespoons melted fat
½ cup sour milk
Grated rind of ½ orange
1 tablespoon fresh orange juice

Mix soda, ginger, and salt with flour and add the other ingredients. Beat thoroughly and pour into a well-greased mold. Steam 50 minutes. Present with a generous serving of orange sauce.

Orange Sauce

1 cup brown sugar
2 tablespoons flour
1½ cups boiling water
1 tablespoon butter
Grated rind of one large orange

Mix sugar and flour. Slowly add boiling water, return to heat, and boil till thickened. Add butter and orange rind. Serve hot.

Plum Pudding — Mrs. O.

115 WEST ORMSBY AVENUE
LOUISVILLE, KY.

½ cup butter
1 cup common molasses
1 " boiling hot coffee (strong)
mix these three

Mix floured
1 lb. raisins
¼ " citron cut fine
1 good size nut-meg
1 large teaspoon cinnamon
½ teaspoon ground cloves
10 cts. blanched almonds
10 cts. candied cherries
flour enough for cake ba[tter]
1 teaspoonful soda
Stew over clean water 2½
(add butter last.)

Mrs. Pope's Plum Pudding

Flour
1 pound raisins
¼ pound citron, finely cut
1 small box candied cherries
½ cup butter
1 cup boiling strong coffee
1 cup common molasses
1 large nutmeg, grated
1 large teaspoon cinnamon
½ teaspoon cloves
1 teaspoon soda
¼ pound almonds, blanched

Mix flour with raisins, citron, and cherries a day in advance of mixing cake. Mix butter, coffee, and molasses; add all dry ingredients and just enough flour to make the consistency of regular cake batter. Mix well and pour into a pan lined with paper and greased. Cook in steamer over hot water for 2½ hours. To reheat, place pan in steamer. Serve with hard sauce flooded with enough whiskey to taste.

Hard Sauce with Cream

4 tablespoons butter
1 cup powdered sugar
1 teaspoon vanilla
1 tablespoon brandy or whiskey
½ cup cream, whipped

Stir butter until creamy and add remaining ingredients. Serve very cold.

Note: Miss Jennie's files contain two copies of this recipe, both on Mrs. Pope's stationery but each with a different Louisville address heading. One simply lists her address as "Upper River Road," while the other is more exact: "115 West Ormsby Avenue." The envelope with the former address is postmarked December 20, 1920.

Snowballs

⅓ cup butter, softened
½ cup sugar
½ cup flour
½ cup cornstarch
2 teaspoons baking powder
⅔ cup milk
3 egg whites, beaten stiff
Powdered sugar

Cream butter and sugar. Sift together flour, cornstarch, and baking powder and combine with butter mixture. Slowly add the milk and then fold in the egg whites; mix thoroughly. Pour into well-buttered baking cups or individual molds filled about ⅔ full and steam for 30 minutes. Turn out gently and roll in powdered sugar. Serve with fruit sauce (page 152), if desired.

Note: These are tasty (and pretty) served in a pool of raspberry sauce.

Pineapple Pudding

2 3/4 cups of scalded cream
1/3 cup of corn starch
1/4 teaspoonful of salt
1/4 cup of cold milk
1/4 " " sugar
1 can of grated pineapple
whites of 3 eggs, beaten stiff.

Mix the corn starch, sugar, salt, and cold milk well, and add to the scalded cream in a double boiler, stir constantly until it thickens. Cook from [illegible] to fifteen minutes, add eggs, then pineapple. Mold, congeal and serve with whipped cream.

Pineapple Pudding

2¾ cups cream, scalded
⅓ cup corn starch
¼ cup sugar
¼ teaspoonful salt
¼ cup cold milk
1 can grated pineapple
3 egg whites, stiffly beaten

Combine the cornstarch, salt, and sugar; add to the scalded cream in a double boiler, stirring constantly until thickened (10 to 15 minutes). Then add egg whites and pineapple. Pour into molds and allow to congeal. Serve with whipped cream.

Woodford Pudding

¾ cup butter, beaten until very light
1 cup sugar
1½ cups flour
1 cup blackberry jam
3 eggs, separated
3 tablespoonfuls sour cream or buttermilk
1 nutmeg, grated
1 teaspoonful soda

Mix all ingredients except egg whites. Pour into a greased mold or dish and bake until a pick inserted into the center comes out clean. After baking, beat the egg whites with a little sugar (¼ - ½ cup). Dollop meringue onto top of pudding and brown lightly. Serve with a pudding sauce.

This recipe is a variation of one that probably originated long ago in Woodford County, Kentucky. Jennie had close ties in that county, whose seat is Versailles, as her maternal grandfather's extensive farm lay in both Franklin and Woodford Counties. Jennie's mother, Ella Scott Green, was born and grew up on that farm known as Locust Hill and later also as Scotland, located only five miles from downtown Frankfort. Their beautiful Greek Revival house, built in 1847, is still occupied and stands just off Interstate 64 east of Frankfort.

Cream Brandy Pudding Sauce

1 cup sugar
1 cup water
3 egg yolks
2 tablespoons brandy
½ cup cream
Dash of salt

Cook sugar and water until it threads. Beat remaining ingredients together and then add syrup slowly, stirring constantly until thick.

Fruit Sauce

½ cup sugar
1 cup water
½ can apricots, peaches, or strawberries, or ½ cup fruit juice or syrup, currant, raspberry, orange, or pineapple
1 tablespoon arrowroot
¼ cup water

Boil sugar and water together 5 minutes. Add fruit or fruit juice of choice and bring to a boil, and if using the fruit, press through a sieve. Serve warm or hot, as desired.

Miscellaneous Sweets

Maple Macaroon Soufflé

1 cup milk, scalded
½ cup macaroons, crumbled
3 eggs, separated
½ teaspoon maple flavoring
½ cup ground nuts

Combine milk and macaroons; pour slowly into the beaten egg yolks. Allow to cool and add flavoring. Beat egg whites till stiff and fold them into milk mixture. Bake in an oiled 9-inch mold in a moderate oven for 20 to 30 minutes, or until firm. When done, place mold in hot water for 20 minutes; then turn out and sprinkle with ground nuts. Serve at once with whipped cream.

Cream Taffy

2 cups granulated sugar
½ teacup water
½ teaspoon cream of tartar
2 tablespoons vinegar
1 tablespoon vanilla, peppermint, or any desired flavoring
1 tablespoon butter

Use enough of the water to wet the sugar; add cream of tartar and vinegar. Stir lightly over fire until the mixture boils. Boil until the syrup will harden but not be brittle when tried in cold water. Remove from fire and add desired flavoring. Pour into buttered tin and cool. *As soon as it can be handled, pull until white and glossy. Cut in pieces. Candy will require several hours to develop the cream texture.

Note: On the back of this recipe Miss Jennie noted the recipe's cookbook source, ending with, "Be sure to get." That book, *Treasures of a Hundred Cooks,* was among the few in her collection!
*The cookbook includes here a step Miss Jennie omitted: "As edges cool, fold toward center."

Dear Miss Jennie -

Lillian said she hoped you could make them out - as she didn't make hers by a receipt -

Sincerely -

Lula B

HARDINSBURG JAN 9 AM 1926

2 CENTS UNITED STATES POSTAGE

Miss Jennie Green -
Falls of Rough -

Cups of Sugar.

Cup Water.

1 table spoon Vinegar

2

teaspoon salt

able spoons Cream

ok 'till makes soft taf

hen put in water and

ll to cup before

eating - Drop them

om pan & dip in

elted Chocolate -

Lillian's Chocolate Dipped Cream Candies

4 cups sugar
1 cup water
1½ tablespoons vinegar
1 teaspoon salt
3 tablespoons cream
Bitter chocolate, melted

Cook all ingredients except chocolate to the soft-ball stage. Allow to cool and beat until very stiff. Drop from spoon and dip in bitter chocolate.

Minted Nuts

1 cup sugar
½ cup water
1 tablespoon light corn syrup
⅛ teaspoon salt
6 marshmallows
½ teaspoon essence of peppermint or 3 drops oil of peppermint
3 cups walnut halves

Cook together slowly sugar, water, corn syrup, and salt. Remove from heat just before it forms a soft ball when a little is dropped into cold water, or to 230° F. with a candy thermometer. Add marshmallows; stir until they are melted. Add peppermint and nuts and stir with circular motion until every nut is coated and mixture hardens. Cool on unglazed paper. These will keep fresh in tightly covered jar for at least a week.

Pulled Molasses Candy

1 cup molasses
2 cups brown sugar
1 cup water
3 tablespoons vinegar
3 tablespoons butter

Mix molasses, sugar, water, and vinegar in a sauce pan. Bring to a boil and cook until very brittle when a small amount is dropped into cold water. Add butter and pour onto buttered plate. Butter hands and pull!!

Old-Fashioned Molasses Candy

3 tablespoonfuls butter
2 cups molasses
⅔ cup sugar
1 tablespoonful cider vinegar

An iron or copper kettle with round bottom is best for making this. Put butter in, place over fire and when melted add molasses and sugar. Stir until sugar is dissolved–doing this well when the candy is nearly done lest it burn. Boil until the mixture becomes brittle in cold water. Add vinegar just before taking it from the fire, and then pour into a well-buttered pan. When cool enough to handle, pull until light in color and porous in quality; do this with the tips of the fingers and thumbs. Cut in small pieces with greased shears and then arrange on slightly buttered platters to cool.

Peppermint Ice cream

10¢ red stick candy
1 pt fresh milk heat
until warm
dissolve 1 tablespoon gela in
warm water
1 qt cream
put candy in milk
dissolve then strain

Peppermint Ice Cream

1 pint fresh milk
10 sticks red peppermint candy
1 tablespoon unflavored gelatin
1 quart cream

Heat milk until warm, then add candy and allow it to dissolve. When dissolved, strain the milk mixture to remove any remaining particles. Dissolve gelatin in ¼ cup of warm water. Add cream and dissolved gelatin to the milk and blend well. Freeze according to ice cream freezer instructions.

Kay Stanton was a child of only three or four years when Miss Jennie visited her parents' home to examine their new electric food freezer, a purchase Jennie was considering. As she stood in the basement where the freezer was located, Kay's perspective left her with lasting impressions of green shoes as they deliberately descended the basement steps.

Graham Beard, a college student and luncheon or dinner guest of Jennie in 1958, wrote in his thank-you note: "It was great to actually have some real ice cream for a change." The fact that the note's date is February 7 shows just how fond Jennie was of ice cream.

Ice Cream Cones

½ cupful powdered sugar
¼ cupful butter
¼ cupful sweet milk
1 teacupful flour
½ teaspoonful vanilla

Cream sugar and butter till light; stir in milk, flour, and vanilla. Turn into a lightly greased shallow baking pan. Spread smooth with a cake turner or broad knife. Bake to a light brown, and while still warm, cut into squares and roll into a cone or cornucopia. Pinch the lower end of each cone tight so that it will hold the cream. If they cool too quickly, set in the oven to soften enough to permit handling. Cool well before filling.

Rice Milk

Pick and wash half a pint of rice, and boil it in a quart of water till it is quite soft. Then drain it, and mix it with a quart of rich milk. You may add half a pound of whole raisins. Set it over hot coals, and stir it frequently till it boils. When it boils hard, stir in alternately two beaten eggs, and four large table-spoonfuls of brown sugar. Let it continue boiling five minutes longer; then take it from the coals, and send it to table hot. If you put in raisins you must let it boil till they are quite soft.

In a letter to her own mother in the mid 1880s, Jennie's mother exclaimed that her "boys" liked rice. (At the time her sons were about 14, 7 and 2 years old.)

Lemon Cream

12 lady fingers (see Cookies and Small Cakes)
Sherry
4 egg-yolks
5 tablespoons sugar
Juice and rind of 1 lemon, grated
3 tablespoons hot water
4 egg whites
2 tablespoons sugar

Line a dish with the lady fingers and sprinkle with sherry. Cook next four ingredients together until thick. Beat egg whites and sugar until stiff and fold into first mixture. Pour into dish with lady fingers and serve cold.

Note: Jennie's *X* marks this recipe, which shows much use.

Orange Caramel

Pare 6 oranges, removing membrane with peel, and cut crosswise, in slices. Put ½ cup sugar and ½ cup water in a small saucepan, and boil quickly until syrup is a golden brown. Arrange layer of orange slices in glass dish; sprinkle with sugar; pour over enough of the syrup to form a thin coating over the orange; add another layer of orange and syrup; repeat until entire orange is used. Beat ½ cup cream until stiff, pile lightly on the orange, and sprinkle with chopped walnuts.

Apple Crystals

3 cups granulated sugar
1½ cups water
3 red apples (peeled, cored, and quartered)

Mix sugar and water; stir over low fire until sugar is dissolved and then bring to boiling. Cut each apple quarter into 3 slices and drop all slices into the boiling syrup. Cook gently until slices are transparent. Remove from syrup and arrange on wax paper; allow to stand 24 hours in a cool, dry place. Next, roll each slice in granulated sugar and roll twice again at 24-hour intervals. After third rolling, allow the crystals to stand until they are so dry that no moisture exudes from them. Pack carefully into flat boxes and keep in a cool dry place until ready to use. This amount of syrup will make 5 dozen crystals, 1 dozen at a time. (One-fourth cup hot water may be added to the syrup, if needed.) If properly dried and then stored in an airtight container, this confection keeps well for many weeks.

KITCHEN HINTS

SALADS

*A piece of garlic added to the French dressing greatly enhances the flavor.
*That discolored line between the white and yolk of a hard-boiled egg will be avoided if eggs are plunged into cold water the instant they are taken from the stove.
*A leftover egg yolk may be dropped into a pan of boiling water to which one teaspoon of salt has been added for each quart of water. Remove the water from the fire so that it will no longer boil. Cool the hard-boiled yolk and use in green salads or sieve for topping cooked greens.
*To revive wilted lettuce or other salad greens, put them in a pan of ice water to which has been added a cupful of vinegar. Let them set for half an hour and they will be quite crisp. Also, wrap lettuce in a damp towel and stick the ends of the towel in a dish of water to keep it fresh for days.
*Cheese will never get mouldy if the cut part is rubbed with butter and covered with waxed paper or wrapped in a cloth which has been dipped in vinegar.

*Use muffin pans to mold the salad; they make just the right individual proportions, and save space in the icebox, too.
*It is simple enough to clean vinegar cruets by filling them with warm water to which a few drops of household ammonia have been added. Let stand about an hour; then rinse with lukewarm water.

VEGETABLES

*To prevent cabbage or greens of any kind from boiling over, add a piece of butter the size of a walnut and they can be left quite safely.
*A very little vinegar or lemon juice added to the water will improve the color of cauliflower.
*Water for cooking vegetables should be boiling before they are added. This helps shorten the time of boiling. One-half teaspoon of salt to one quart of water may be added in the middle of the cooking period. This gives a better flavor than if it is added after the vegetables are cooked.
*While cooking, cover all vegetables grown under the ground and leave uncovered all that grow above the ground. There is less odor and they cook better.
*An added slice of raw potato will absorb some of the salt if too much has been used in a dish.
*Thick sour cream seasoned lightly with salt and pepper makes a good sauce for hot, buttered beets. Mix just before serving.
*Asparagus cooked uncovered will retain its natural green color.
*In frying potatoes, it will be found that they brown much more quickly if the slices are dredged with flour before immersing in the boiling fat.
*Butter the bean-pot before cooking the beans and see how much easier it will wash.

Main Dishes

*To help brown a pot roast, mix a tablespoon of granulated sugar in with the fat or meat drippings used for searing the roast. The sugar gives a brown color and very good flavor to the stock and gravy.
*Next time when making gravy, mix the salt with the flour and this will prevent lumping.
*An excellent coloring medium for gravies is strong cold tea. Many people prefer this to the usual burnt sugar and water, as the tea colors without giving the sweet taste which is to many people so objectionable.
*Tough meat can be made tender if placed in vinegar water for a few minutes, or you may add a little lemon juice to the water in which it is boiled.
*Plenty of pinfeathers on a goose is an indication that the bird will be tender.
*Try baking slices of ham in pineapple juice.
*A little peanut butter added to beef stew gives it a delightful new flavor.
*Cover the pan in which you are cooking dumplings with a glass pie plate, and you will be able to see whether the water is boiling properly without removing the cover.

Breads

*One teaspoon lemon juice added to either waffle or fritter batter improves the flavor and makes it more crisp.
*Fine salt rubbed on the griddle will often prevent pancakes sticking.
*Keep a soft pastry brush with fine bristles to clean the difficult corners of the electric toaster. It will sweep out all the crumbs so hard to get at.
*When making butter balls with boxwood paddles, soak paddles in iced water 15 minutes before starting to make the balls. Keep the iced water convenient and dip in the paddles frequently, as this prevents the butter

from sticking. About ⅔ of a tablespoon of butter is required for each ball.
*If milk is scalded and kept in a shallow basin, it will remain sweet for a longer time than if kept in a deep jug.
*To remove brown marks from dishes caused by baking in the oven, rub them well with common salt.
*One hates to have a new oven become brown and stained. After it has been used, open wide the doors and allow it to cool thoroughly before closing up.

Cakes

*To many would-be cake bakers, the greatest difficulty is the creaming of the butter and sugar. The easiest method is to do it with a wire potato masher, the work being accomplished in a quarter of the usual time.
*A teaspoon of vinegar added to boiled frosting when the flavoring is added will give the icing a creamy texture.
*To keep cakes fresh, dip a small table napkin in cold water, wring out, and put in the tin where cakes are stored. If this is renewed occasionally, it will be found that the cakes keep for a long time.
*A little cold water added when creaming butter and sugar for a cake will make the creaming easier.
*Dried fruits will not stick to the food chopper if the chopper is first rinsed with boiling water.

Pies

*A pinch of soda added to beaten egg whites to be used for meringue will issue a good stiff topping.
*A good way to make pies more attractive is to brush the top crust with a

mixture of milk and sugar just before putting them in the oven. However, they brown more quickly with this finish and require closer watching.
*Equal parts of whipped cream and white cream cheese with a dash of cinnamon and cloves make an extra fine topping for warm plum or apple cobbler.
*In handling pastry, work quickly with a light touch and use as little extra flour as possible.
*Meringue falls when the oven is too hot. Always have the oven at less than moderate heat.

DESSERTS, ETCETERA

*A mashed banana well mixed in the white of an egg that has been beaten until stiff makes a good substitute for whipped cream.
*When custards are cooking, very often a thin skin forms on top which is rather tough. This can be remedied by placing a cloth or paper over the top during the cooling process.
*If the egg beater works a little hard when whipping cream, lubricate it with glycerine. There will be no danger of aftertaste in the cream.
*In making a soufflé add a pinch of soda to the beaten egg white. This helps to keep it fluffy and puffy.
*A few cloves put on top of jelly will prevent mold.
*A seed placed in the bottom of the jar when canning peaches will improve the flavor of the fruit.
*For the children's party: elephants, tigers, lions, camels, and horses besides dogs and cats all marching across the table are a delight. And it is not at all hard to accomplish. Take animal crackers, dip the feet of each one in thick icing made by moistening confectioner's sugar with a little cream and stand them on vanilla wafers. If they are a bit wabbly, the white of an egg will glue them fast. Besides eatable, they make attractive place cards, or center table decorations.

Household Hints

Decorating

*Re-curling ostrich feathers is something we all have to do occasionally. The best way to do this is to sprinkle a little salt over the feather before attempting to curl it; then hold it over a register or radiator until it is full of hot air, and then draw each tendril carefully over a blunt paper knife, or case knife. Don't curl them too tightly, as it is better to do them often, and so let them have the soft, drooping effect, so much more desirable than the tight curl.

*If your windows are small and your ceiling low, the effect of height and length may be gained if the over-drapes on your curtains are allowed to come to the floor.

*Cut flowers will keep longer in water that has been slightly salted.

*A teaspoonful of caster oil applied to the roots of your ferns and palms

every three months is a marvelous stimulant for their growth and beauty.
*When rugs have become limp, or curled, try coating the under side with a very thin cooked starch.

Personal

*Immediately after dishwashing, drop a little lemon juice in the palms and rub well over hands to keep them soft and white.
*When the bristles of a hairbrush become soft, stiffen them in the following manner: Wash the brush well in about a quart of hot water to which a dessertspoonful of ammonia has been added. Then dissolve a large lump of salt in cold water; dip the brush in several times, and leave to dry in the open air.
*For falling hair use castor oil and bay rum in equal proportions. It should be well rubbed into the roots of the hair with the tips of the fingers.
*For oily skin, try putting half a lemon into the water jug; the water and lemon should be changed every two or three days. Dry the face thoroughly after using this wash.

General

*To tell the difference between porcelain and pottery, hold the article in the light. If transparent it is porcelain. Pottery is opaque and not so hard and white as porcelain.
*Kerosene oil is a sure remedy for red ants. Place small blocks under a sugar barrel, so as not to let the oil touch the barrel.
*Cayenne pepper will keep the store-room and pantry free from ants and cockroaches.
*Turpentine is a sure preventive against moths. By dropping a trifle in drawers, trunks, and cupboards, it will render the garments secure from injury during the summer months. It will also keep ants from storerooms

and closets if a few drops are put in the corners and upon shelves. It is sure destruction to all sorts of vermin and will drive them away from various articles of furniture. It does not injure either furniture or clothing. One tablespoon added to a bucket of warm water is excellent for cleaning painted woodwork.

*Charcoal and quicklime are the best purifiers for musty places. To use charcoal, suspend it in net bags. Make a large number of bags to hold several large lumps of charcoal. These will absorb all sorts of bad odors and leave the atmosphere pure and sweet. Restore the charcoal each week by putting the lumps in a fire pot and heating very hot. The freshened lumps will then serve a new period of usefulness.

*A little powdered starch placed under the paper in a drawer will free it from dampness.

*Paint brush marks on glass, such as the splashes left by careless workmen on window panes, can be scraped off with a penny dipped in cold water.

*Paint may be removed from windows with hot vinegar.

*Paint brushes which have hardened with paint may be restored by boiling in vinegar for a few minutes and then rinsing in clear water.

*If the feet or rockers of chairs are waxed they will not mar the floors.

*A clothespin placed on each side of the clothes prop will keep it from slipping on the wire clothesline.

*Two thicknesses of cotton batting make an excellent pad for an ironing board.

*It is very desirable to keep borax in the house. Its effect is to soften the hardest water, and it is excellent for cleansing the hair. Some washerwomen use it for a washing powder, instead of soda, in boiling water, and they save in soap nearly half, whilst the borax, being a neutral salt, does not injure the texture of the linen.

*To set colors, wash in strong salt or alum water; also, a teacup of lye in a pail of water will improve black calicoes.

*To set different colors in fabrics: for blue, use a handful of salt; for reds and pinks, a little vinegar; for green, a lump of alum; for tan or linen color, a little hay water; for gray or brown, use ox gall.

*Fabrics to be dyed will be more satisfactory if they are washed first in warm water to which has been added two tablespoons household ammonia to each gallon of water

*Make a comfortable pair of shoes waterproof for outdoor use by melting together a dressing of two parts of beeswax to one part of mutton fat. Apply at night and in the morning; wipe well before wearing with a piece of flannel.

*To make the lamps burn brightly, soak the wicks in vinegar before using, and put a pinch of salt into the oil as well. Every part of the burner should be well washed and brushed as often as once a week.

*When a wick refuses to go into the burner of your oil stove, wax with beeswax the narrow sides, ends and flat sides of the wick, particularly the ends which go into the burner. You will have no more trouble.

*When screws keep working loose, remove, dip the tip in glue and replace at once. They seldom work out again.

*To remove a rusty screw, first heat the screw driver and then apply to the screw, when it will easily turn.

*Coal should be kept in a dry airy place. It will burn longer and make a brighter fire than when kept in a close cellar without ventilation.

*A good way to use up coal dust is to take a shovelful and before placing it on the fire sprinkle a little fine soda on it. This enables it to burn well and brightly.

*A few drops of lavender added to the ink will make your whole desk fragrant.

*When a globe, tumbler, or any other piece of glass drops and shatters, do not try to pick or brush the fragments up, but dampen a piece of woolen

cloth and pat gently. This will gather up the smallest particles without a particle of danger.

Household Cleaning

Fabrics

*Before sweeping carpets, sprinkle them with a little moist salt. This will restore the colors and renew the brightness, and also lay the dust during the process of sweeping. Moist tealeaves can also be used in the same manner.
*When soot falls on the carpet or rug, never attempt to sweep it up at once, for the result is sure to be a disfiguring mark. Cover it thickly with well-dried salt, which will enable it to be swept up cleanly and the slightest stain will go.
*Corn meal is an excellent cleaning agent, especially for flannel articles. When added to lemon juice, it may be used in whitening hats, shoes, or other items. If a rug is particularly dusty, sprinkle it with corn meal and then sweep. You will be surprised at the amount of dirt it will remove.
*Ammonia will take grease spots from almost every fabric. Put on the ammonia nearly clear. Lay blotting paper on the place, and press a hot flat-iron on it for a few moments. A few drops of it will clean and whiten laces, also muslins.
*To prevent fruit stains from being permanent, wet the stained spot with whiskey before sending it to wash, and there will be no sign of it when the article comes in.
*Scorch, perspiration, and other stains on white silk can be removed with bicarbonate of soda mixed to a paste with cold water.
*To remove iron rust, fruit or ink stains, rub the spots well with lemon,

then cover with salt and place in the sun. Repeat process if necessary.
*To bleach linen or muslin, moisten with lemon juice and spread on the grass in the sun.
*A little vinegar added to the last rinsing water when washing colored clothes will revive their natural shades.
*New silk stockings should be washed in tepid water and rubbed with a mild soap before wearing. After washing them, give them a final rinsing in clean water, to which a little vinegar has been added. This will remove any trace of soap and preserve the silk.
*Clean your felt hats with a dry sponge—a regular soft sponge. Rub it briskly over the felt and all dust and grime will gradually disappear.
*To rejuvenate soiled dancing slippers, apply wood alcohol with a cloth, rubbing the same way as the satin. This will restore them to nearly normal even when they seem too shabby to wear again.
*Black goods that have grown grayish can often be freshened by wiping off with alcohol. This is particularly good for black hats and does not hurt crepe if properly applied.

Floors

*Tiled floors or hearths that have become stained can be cleaned by rubbing with a cloth dipped in kerosene and a little lard. Wipe afterwards with a soft, dry cloth.
*To make red tiles a nice, bright, clear color rub well with a lemon dipped in fine salt. Leave it on for a few minutes, then wash in the usual way. You will find this well worth the trouble, for when it is finished the tiles will be a nice clear red, with all stains removed.
*To remove grease spots from the floor, sprinkle them with dry soda, pour over this boiling water, let stand a short time, scrub, and spot is gone.
*Don't use a stiff brush when washing linoleum. This destroys the lustre. Wash lightly with soap and water.

Furniture

*Walnut furniture can be cleaned with a piece of flannel dipped in paraffin.

*Hot camphorated oil applied with a soft flannel will often remove white spots on furniture caused by water or resulting from hot dishes being placed directly on the table. It may require a couple of applications, but in ordinary cases it will be perfectly successful.

*To remove scratches on furniture, dip a woolen rag in boiled linseed oil, and with it well rub the scratched article, which should then be varnished with shellac dissolved in alcohol.

*A simple way to cover scratches on a polished wood surface is to thoroughly rub the meat of a pecan nut into the scratch.

*Before applying polish to furniture, it should be wiped with a cloth wrung out of lukewarm water to which a little vinegar has been added. This cleans the wood, allowing a more brilliant polish.

*To remove fuzz on table, cover the spot with lemon oil, then gently rub off with a soft cloth. The spot should then be rubbed briskly and polished with a furniture dressing.

*To clean piano keys, rub lightly with soft cloth moistened with alcohol. If slightly yellowed, dampen clean dry cloth with peroxide of hydrogen and rub over keys.

*A useful polish for mahogany is made of olive oil and vinegar; two tablespoonfuls of oil to a dessertspoonful of vinegar. Mix well, apply with an old flannel and polish.

*A solution made of one quart of boiling water, three tablespoons of linseed oil and one tablespoon of turpentine is excellent for washing furniture. Wash one section at a time with a soft piece of flannel dipped in the solution and then dry the furniture with cheesecloth.

*A dustless dustcloth can be made from a piece of cheesecloth immersed two hours in hot soapsuds to which a few drops of turpentine have been added.

*Leather chair coverings should occasionally be rubbed with linseed oil and vinegar to freshen the leather and to prevent cracking. Mix together two parts boiled linseed oil with one part vinegar. Use very little, and the leather must afterward be rubbed with soft dusters till the polish is restored.

Miscellaneous

*For washing windows, mirrors, or glassware a little ammonia or vinegar added to the water will make the glass sparkle brightly. Also, a few drops on a piece of paper will take off every spot or finger mark on the glass.
*Gilt frames which have become dusty or fly-specked can be renovated by a careful dusting followed by washing with one ounce of soda beaten up with the whites of three eggs.
*After juice has been extracted, dip lemon rinds in salt to clean tarnished copper or brass.
*Oil paintings can be cleaned with a pure white soap and water with a little care. Any other treatment should be undertaken by an expert.
*Clean mother-of-pearl handles or other articles of the same material by applying pure olive oil and rubbing with a nail brush, followed by a rubbing with a piece of chamois.
*A cloth dampened with alcohol will clean dusty candles without taking off the luster.
*When cleansing the bathtub use a flannel rag dipped in kerosene for taking off the first grease and dirt and then give it a good wash with hot water and laundry soap.
*Japanned trays may be cleaned with a mixture of vinegar and powdered whiting. Apply with a soft flannel, wipe off with a clean cloth and polish with chamois.
*To clean feather pillows in a satisfactory manner, first put the pillows into

a large tub and scrub them well with a small brush dipped in a solution of chloride of lime and warm water. Afterward rinse them thoroughly and spread them on the grass to dry, or on tables in the open air, turning them constantly. After two days' treatment in a warm, strong sun, pin the pillows onto a clothesline on every fine or windy day till they are quite dry; then beat with a cane. This will disentangle the feathers and the pillows will be like new.

*Removing dust and dirt from the crevices in Dresden china ornaments is rather difficult. Apply a soap lather with an old shaving brush and you will find that it will reach all the dirt and remove it. Rinse well in clear water.

*Glasses that are stuck together may be separated by filling the top one with cold water and setting the bottom one in hot water.

*To keep silver salt shaker tops from becoming corroded, cover the inside of each with paraffin. While it is cooling, prick holes in the paraffin with a large needle.

*The china breaking hazard will be lowered some by simply slipping a two to three inch piece of rubber hose over the mouth of the water faucet.

*An easy way to clean the inside of an aluminum coffee pot is to slice a lemon and put the slices in the pot with plenty of cold water. Let come to a boil and keep boiling until the inside surface of the pot may be cleaned with a cloth to look like new.

*When washing glassware, do not put it in water bottom first, as it may crack from sudden expansion. Each delicate glass can be safely washed in very hot water if slipped in edgewise.

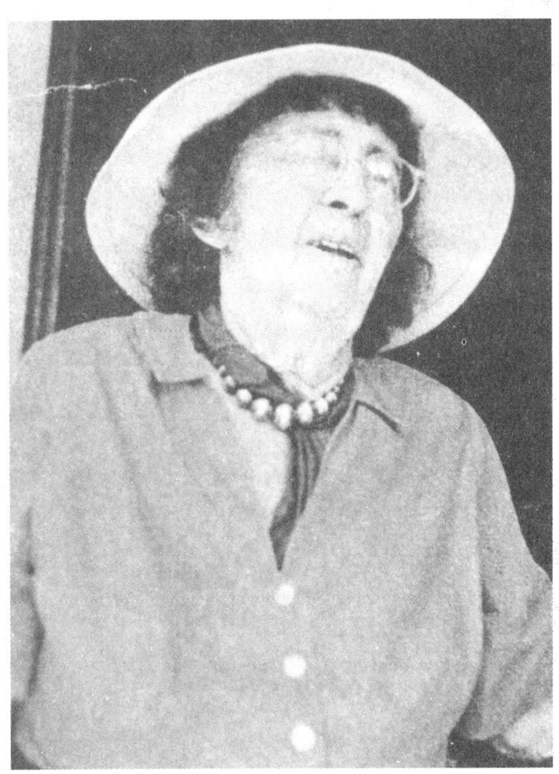

Miss Jennie at age 83

EQUIVALENT TABLES

Oven
Below 300° F.= very slow
300° F.= slow
325° F.= moderately slow
350° F.= moderate
375° F. = moderately hot
400°-425° F. = hot/quick
450°-475° F. = very hot
500° F. = extremely hot

Candy Making
230°-234° F. = Thread
234°-240° F. = Soft Ball
244°-248° F. = Firm Ball
250°-265° F. = Hard Ball
270°-290° F. = Soft Crack
300°-310° F. = Hard Crack

Egg Sizes/Weights
Weight based upon packaged sizing:
Extra large = 2¼ ounces
Large = 2 ounces
Medium = 1¾ ounces
Small = 1½ ounces

Liquid Measures
1 dessertspoon = 1 scant tablespoon
1 wine glass = ¼ cup

1 teacup = ½ cup
1 gill/jill = ½ cup (¼ pint)
1 tumbler = 1 cup
1 large coffeecup = 1 cup
1 cup = 8 ounces
1 pint = 2 cups
1 quart = 2 pints
1 gallon = 4 quarts

Dry Measures

(Note: Dry measure cups, pints, and quarts, are about 1/6 larger than liquid measures of the same terms.)
1 saltspoon = ⅛ teaspoon
1 tablespoon = 3 teaspoons
1 cup = 16 tablespoons
1 pint = 2 cups
1 quart = 2 pints
1 gallon = 4 quarts
1 peck = 2 gallons (approximately 25 medium apples, tomatoes, etc.)
1 bushel = 4 pecks

Weight to Volume Measures

Almonds, blanched–	1 ounce = approximately ⅓-½ cup
Butter–	4 ounces = ¼ pound = 1 stick=8 tablespoons=½ cup
	1 ounce = 2 tablespoons
	the size of an egg = ½ stick=4 tablespoons
	the size of a walnut = 3 tablespoons
Cornmeal–	1 pound = 3 cups
Flour–	1 pound = 4 cups/1 quart

Liquids–	1 pound = 2 cups
Molasses–	12 ounces = 1 cup
	1 pound = 1⅓ cups
Potatoes, white–	1 pound= 4 medium
Spices, ground–	1 ounce = 5 tablespoons
Sugar,	
powdered–	1 pound= 3½ cups
brown–	1 pound= 2⅔ cups
granulated–	1 pound= 2 cups
Tomatoes–	1 pound = 4 medium

Miscellaneous–

1 nutmeg yields approximately 3 teaspoons grated/ground

1 average lemon yields approximately 3 tablespoons juice and 3 teaspoons grated rind

Recipe Index

Appetizers

Breads

Cakes

Candies

Cookies

Desserts (Miscellaneous)

Meats

Beef

Game

Pork

Poultry

Seafood

Muffins

Pies

Puddings (Dessert)

Salads

Sauces

Side Dishes

Vegetables

Inside Miss Jennie's Kitchen

Mail to:

Treetops Enterprises
1715 Stagecoach Rd.
Hanson, KY 42413
For Orders Call:
270-825-1533
Email Orders:
treetops@spis.net

Please send me

____Inside Miss Jennie's Kitchen @19.95 each __________
____The Greens of Falls of Rough @18.95 each __________
Postage & handling* __________
Sub Total __________
KY residents add 6% sales tax __________
Total enclosed __________

* Postage & handling charges - $5.00 for first book and .50¢ for each additional

Make checks or money order to Treetops Enterprises

Ship to:

NAME ____

ADDRESS ____

CITY____________________ STATE________ ZIP ____________